AVIATION LEGENDS PAPER AIRPLANE BOOK

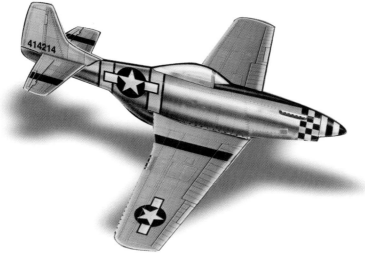

Ken Blackburn and Jeff Lammers

Plane Graphics by Dean Fleming

Workman Publishing, New York

To Lauren, for her invaluable assistance with writing, editing, creating, cutting, folding, throwing, organizing, scheduling, typing, and gluing, and for her willingness to throw paper planes with me around the world and throughout time.

—K. B.

To all the great people who enjoy and enhance the wonderful world of aviation. To Ken Blackburn for all his efforts and creativeness in the paper-model world. And a very special thanks to Jim Daron, who has been a great friend and teacher in my full-scale airplane adventures.

—J. L.

Photo Credits: AASI Aircraft: p.15 (right). **Courtesy Boeing Aircraft:** pp. 8 (top right and middle), 10 (right), 11 (top), 28, 38, 39, 46, 48. **Cessna:** p. 51. **CORBIS:** pp. 5 (right and top), 14 (bottom left and right), 15 (left), 18 (right), 26, 56; Leonard deSelva, pp. 6 (top), 7 (top); Museum of Flight, p. 9 (top); John H. Clark, pp. 10 (1963), 11 (bottom); Roger Ressmeyer, p. 11 (1986); Rykoff Collection, p. 12 (1961); Paul A. Sauders, p. 13 (top); EyeUbiquitous, p. 18 (left); George Hall, p. 19; Lake County Museum, p. 31 (left); James Sugar, p. 55. **Culver Pictures:** pp. 4 (1853), 5 (1907 and 1910), 7 (1926), 12 (left and 1896), 13 (1912 and 1941), 23. **Delta Airlines:** p. 27. **Edwards Air Force Base:** p. 36. **Hulton Archive by Getty:** pp. 5 (left), 6 (1911), 30. **Marshall Space Flight Center:** p. 4 (1200). **NASA:** pp. 11 (1969), 12 (right), 35, 40, 54, 58. **National Archives:** p. 9 (1945). **New Jersey Aviation Hall of Fame:** pp.7 (bottom and 1923), 8 (1932 and 1933), 9 (1939), 10 (left and 1953), 22. **New York Public Library:** pp. 4 (top), 8 (left), 14 (top). **Paul Dopper:** p. 32. **Photo Vault:** pp. 31 (right), 42, 43, 44. **United States Air Force:** pp. 34, 47.

Copyright © 2001 by Ken Blackburn and Jeff Lammers
Plane graphics copyright © 2001 by Dean Fleming

Renderings on page 62 by Matthew Fox.

Library of Congress Cataloging-in-Publication Data

Blackburn, Ken.
    Aviation legends paper airplane book / by Ken Blackburn and Jeff Lammers ; plane graphics by Dean Fleming
        p. cm.
    ISBN 0-7611-2376-8 (alk. paper)
    1. Paper airplanes 2. Airplanes—History. I. Lammers, Jeff. II. Title.
    TL778 .B55 2001
    745.592—dc21   2001045431

Workman books are available at special discount when purchased in bulk for special premiums and sales promotions as well as for fund-raising or educational use. Special editions or book excerpts can also be created to specification. For details, contact the Special Sales Director at the address below.

Workman Publishing Company, Inc.

708 Broadway, New York, NY 10003-9555

www.workman.com

Printed in the United States of America

First Printing October 2001
10 9 8 7 6 5 4 3 2

Contents

History of Aviation

EARLY ATTEMPTS

Although mankind has mastered flight only in the last hundred years, humans have been attempting to emulate the birds for centuries. Some have even strapped on wings and jumped from great heights, only to learn the hard way that there is a lot more to flying than simply flapping your arms.

The first flying machines to be historically documented were kites, which were built in China over two thousand years ago.

Montgolfier brothers' hot air balloon

Large enough to carry people into the sky, they were used mainly by armies for keeping tabs on enemy movements. There is no evidence, though, of these early kites evolving into true gliders. In fact, the first machines to fly without being tethered to the ground did not even have wings.

In November 1783, François Pilatre de Rozier and the Marquis d'Arlandes became the first people to take to the air in a balloon, which was built in

Flight Fact: Before the Montgolfier brothers allowed humans to go up in their balloon, they tested for the potential dangers of altitude by sending aloft a rooster, a duck, and a sheep. All three survived just fine.

France by the Montgolfier brothers and used hot air for lift. The first hydrogen-filled balloon took flight, also in France, just a few days later. By the 1800s, balloons were being used around the world, not only by civilians for recreation, but also by the military for reconnaissance and for aiming artillery. The next significant development, pioneered in 1852 by French engineer Henri Giffard, was the airship, or blimp—a powered balloon capable of being steered in any direction. While airships continued to grow and evolve through the late 1930s, the crash of the *Hindenburg* in 1937, dramatically captured on film,

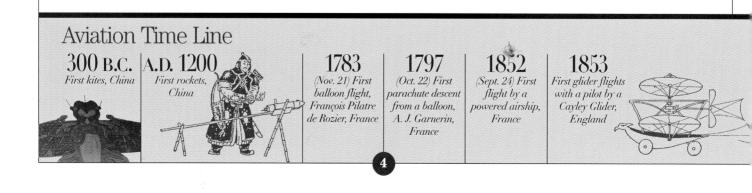

Aviation Time Line

300 B.C.	A.D. 1200	1783	1797	1852	1853
First kites, China	First rockets, China	(Nov. 21) First balloon flight, François Pilatre de Rozier, France	(Oct. 22) First parachute descent from a balloon, A. J. Garnerin, France	(Sept. 24) First flight by a powered airship, France	First glider flights with a pilot by a Cayley Glider, England

The German airship Hindenberg *burst into flames on May 6, 1937 while landing in New Jersey, killing 36 passengers.*

understandably dampened the public's enthusiasm for this form of transport. The crucial factor that ended the need for airships, though, was the emergence of the airplane.

Otto Lilienthal aloft in one of his famous early gliders

The first piloted winged aircraft was a glider created by Sir George Cayley in 1853. Cayley established the importance of stability, control, and balance, proving among other things that it was not necessary for wings to flap in order to enable flight. In the years to follow, several people expanded on Cayley's ideas. The most prolific glider designer and pilot by the end of the 1800s was the German Otto Lilienthal, who logged thousands of flights in the eighteen different gliders he designed. He also made a significant contribution to the history of flying with *Bird Flight as the Basis of Aviation.* The book inspired many people, including two young brothers from Dayton, Ohio, who would change the course of aviation history.

Orville and Wilbur Wright

The Wright brothers picked up where Lilienthal left off at his death. Recognizing that Lilienthal's method of controlling his gliders was inadequate—he would simply shift his weight as a means of directing the glider up or down, left or right—the Wrights systematically

1903
(Dec. 17) Wright brothers make the first controlled flight by a powered airplane, U.S.A.

1906
(Nov. 12) Alberto Santos-Dumont becomes the first person to fly an airplane in Europe

1907
(Nov. 13) First helicopter "hop," by Paul Cornu, France

1909
(July 25) First flight across English Channel, by Louis Bleriot

1910
(Mar. 28) First flight from water, Henri Fabre, France

5

Alberto Santos Dumont's 1906 flight

anyone else in the world had made a powered flight—the Wrights had covered distances up to twenty-four miles in flights lasting up to thirty minutes.

The next pilot to take to the skies—or at least leave the ground—was the Brazilian-born Alberto Santos-Dumont, who flew his plane, *14bis,* a grand total of twenty-three feet on September 13, 1906. Although several European would-be aviators made modest hops, no one aside from the Wrights did any true flying until 1908, when the brothers demonstrated their Model A in Europe and sparked a flurry of aircraft production. By 1910, small aircraft were being manufactured by Bleriot and Voisin in France and Wright and Curtiss in the United States, and performance had improved enough to allow flights across the English Channel and over the Alps.

Flight Fact: The first passenger airline service flew between Tampa and St. Petersburg, Florida, in 1914. It carried exactly one passenger.

devised flight controls that changed the angle of the wings and tail as a means of guiding their craft. (Remarkably, the system of controls they developed is still in use today.) The Wrights applied their new principles to a series of gliders, making over two thousand flights before attempting to add an engine. Since no lightweight engines or propellers existed, the brothers developed their own, achieving considerable success—their propeller was nearly as efficient as any modern-day design. On December 17, 1903, in an airplane aptly named the *Flyer* (see page 14), the Wright brothers made four short flights that inaugurated the era of powered aviation. They improved on their original design in 1904 and again in 1905 with the *Flyer III,* which is regarded as the first practical airplane. By 1906—before

THE INFLUENCE OF WAR

From 1914 to 1918, World War I resulted in the transformation of aircraft from slow, frail vehicles into agile, capable fighting machines. The governments of the world began to see the military potential of air power, leading to tremendous progress, particularly in the fields of engine technology and aerodynamics. Although Wright Aircraft had produced the first military airplanes in 1908, only limited numbers of military aircraft existed at the beginning of the war and these were used primarily for reconnaissance. All that changed in 1915, when Germany produced the first purpose-built fighters. Almost immediately, it seemed, all military aircraft were being equipped with guns, leading to the

Aviation Time Line *(continued)*

1911		**1911**	**1914**	**1914**	**1919**	**1922**
(June 18) First air race, the "Circuit of Europe," starting from Paris		*(Sept. 17–Nov. 5) First flight across the U.S., by Calbraith Rodgers in Wright biplane*	*(Jan. 1) First scheduled transport by airplane, Benoist Company in Florida*	*(Aug. 4) Beginning of World War I*	*(June 14–15) First nonstop Atlantic crossing, by John Alcock and Arthur W. Brown, Canada to Ireland*	*(Sept. 4) First crossing of the U.S. in one day, by Jimmy Doolittle in a DH-4B*

emergence of air-to-air combat, or "dogfighting" (see the Fokker Dr.I, page 18). This period also saw the introduction of bombers. Initially, pilots had simply carried bombs on their laps until they reached their target, at which point they would drop them over the side by hand. This rather ineffective procedure was rendered obsolete with the development of large aircraft that could carry multiple bombs and drop them from internal cargo areas known as bomb bays. By the end of the war, over a thousand bombers had been built, with the later models capable of flying more than a thousand miles and carrying 7,500-pound payloads.

After the end of World War I, some of the newly unemployed pilots purchased war surplus aircraft and made a living by "barnstorming." Flying from town to town, they took people for rides, and gave daredevil

After World War I, the Curtiss JN-4 "Jenny" became a popular barnstorming aircraft.

Flight Fact: In the late 1800s, touring theatrical companies were dubbed "barnstormers" because they literally performed in country barns. The nickname eventually came to apply to all touring performers, including stunt pilots.

An actual World War I biplane dogfight in progress

aerobatic performances that afforded many people their first look at an actual aircraft. Other pilots used former military planes to transport mail across the country and around the world. Passenger flight, meanwhile, was neither popular nor profitable: The aircraft were too small, and the people too fearful.

Public awareness of the potential of air travel took a major leap forward in 1927 with Charles Lindbergh's historic flight from New York to Paris in the *Spirit of St. Louis* (see

---

1923
(Jan. 9) First flight of an autogiro, by Juan de la Cierva, Spain

1923
(May 2–3) First nonstop crossing of the U.S., by O. G. Kelly and J. A. MacReady in a Fokker T-2

1926
(Mar. 16) First flight of a liquid-powered rocket, by Robert Goddard in the U.S.

1926
(May 9) First flight over the North Pole, by Richard Byrd

1927
(May 20–21) First nonstop New York-to-Paris flight, by Charles Lindbergh in the Spirit of St. Louis

Helicopter History

Da Vinci's air screw

For centuries, visionaries such as Leonardo Da Vinci dreamed of flying machines comparable to modern helicopters. The first actual examples appeared in France in 1907, but were only capable of small hops off the ground.

A breakthrough came in 1925 when Spaniard Juan de la Cierva created a new type of rotor blade that allowed forward flight. Cierva's aircraft, however, was not a true helicopter but an auto-giro, which used an engine and a propeller similar to that of a conventional airplane, with a wind-milling rotor in place of a wing. The first practical helicopter, the VS-300, was developed by Igor Sikorsky in 1939. The VS-300 looked and behaved like today's helicopters, with a single main rotor and a tail boom with a smaller tail rotor.

Since then, performance has been improved using gas turbine engines, which are lighter and more powerful than their original piston-driven counterparts. Although most helicopters are limited in their maximum speed, the new V-22 Osprey incorporates a tilt rotor which allows it to take off and land vertically but to fly with its rotors tilted

Boeing Apache

forward, airplane-style, increasing its speed and range. Today, military helicopters like the Sikorsky Blackhawk and the Boeing Apache are used for troop transport, rescue, and attack. Civilian models such as the Bell Jetranger and Robinson R-22 serve many functions, including medical transport, sightseeing, police surveillance, and traffic and news reporting.

---

page 22). The first practical passenger airplanes were developed not long after, and included "flying boats." These planes, the largest of which could carry over forty passengers, were designed to land on water, since runways had not yet been built to accommodate aircraft of this size. Also beginning to appear were smaller passenger planes, such as the Ford Tri-Motor and the Douglas DC-3 (see page 26), that could land on existing runways. Aircraft technology advanced rapidly through the 1930s, with alu-

The DC-3 revolutionized air transport.

minum (sturdy yet light) replacing wood and fabric, and one-wing designs replacing the two-wing structures. The airplane was just becoming a commercial success as war clouds began to gather over Europe.

By the late 1930s, Germany and Japan were building their air forces at a feverish pace. When World War II broke out in 1939, Germany's formidable air force, the Luftwaffe, equipped with vast numbers of superior aircraft, overwhelmed the air forces of

---

Aviation Time Line *(continued)*

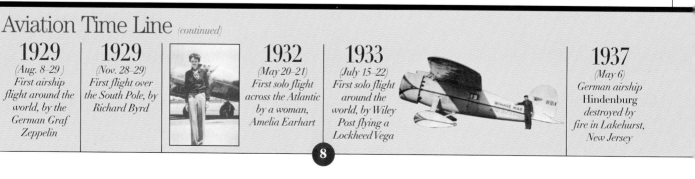

1929
(Aug. 8–29)
First airship flight around the world, by the German Graf Zeppelin

1929
(Nov. 28–29)
First flight over the South Pole, by Richard Byrd

1932
(May 20–21)
First solo flight across the Atlantic by a woman, Amelia Earhart

1933
(July 15–22)
First solo flight around the world, by Wiley Post flying a Lockheed Vega

1937
(May 6)
German airship Hindenburg destroyed by fire in Lakehurst, New Jersey

most of Europe. The following year, Britain's Royal Air Force (RAF) began a desperate attempt to repel the Luftwaffe in what would become known as the Battle of Britain. Production of military aircraft in the United States surged to support the air struggle over Britain, and also to supply aircraft to Russia. On December 14, 1941, Japan bombed Pearl Harbor, launching the United States into battle in the Pacific as well as in Europe. New fighting aircraft such as the P-51 Mustang (see page 30) were quickly developed and produced by the thousands. By 1943, American aircraft manufacturers were turning out planes in record numbers, while the enemy's factories were being bombed. U.S. carrier-based aircraft played a crucial role in turning the tide of the war in the Pacific, devastating Japan's navy at the Battle of Midway. Fast and heavily armored American aircraft such as the Grumman Hellcat and the Vought Corsair began to dominate Japanese fighters such as the Mitsubishi Zero, allowing the American Navy to advance toward Japan. Long-range bombing by B-17s and B-24s in Europe and B-29s in the Pacific crippled the ability of Germany and Japan to continue fighting. The final act of the war occurred in August 1945 when B-29 bombers dropped atomic bombs on Hiroshima and Nagasaki, leading to the Japanese surrender on August 15.

Although jet engines had appeared in experimental German and English planes at the beginning of World War II, the only jet aircraft to play a significant role in the conflict was the German Messerschmitt Me-262, capable of flying 100 m.p.h. faster than its nearest competition. Following the war, the United States and Russia each obtained jet-

Flight Fact: The B-17 bomber nicknamed "Memphis Belle" was completed July 2, 1942, at a cost of $314,109. It became famous for having the first crew to complete twenty-five missions, logged more than 20,000 combat miles, and dropped more than 60 tons of bombs.

Extremely maneuverable, the Mitsubishi Zero was the best Japanese fighter of World War II.

1939
(Aug. 27) First flight by a jet-powered aircraft, the German Heinkel He 178, Germany

1939
(Sept. 2) Beginning of WWII

1945
(Aug. 6) First atomic bomb dropped, from B-29 on Japan

1947
(Oct. 14) First aircraft to exceed the speed of sound, Bell X-1 piloted by Chuck Yeager, U.S.A.

1952
(May 2) First jet-powered airline service, London to Johannesburg

"X" Stands for Experimental

The X planes were created by NASA to research new aircraft technology, beginning with the X-1, which pioneered supersonic flight. A modified

North American X-15

version called the X-1A reached Mach 2.4 in December 1953, and was followed in 1956 by the X-2. Though it reached Mach 3.2, the X-2's instability at this speed resulted in a fatal crash.

The fastest of the group was the North American X-15, which flew to Mach 6.72 (4,530 m.p.h.) and climbed to an altitude of 354,200 feet, or 67 miles. In fact, the X-15 flew high enough to earn three pilots their astronaut's wings. NASA has used these craft to experiment with everything from vertical flight, to wing shapes, to new fighter and rocket technology, and is now at work on the X-45.

The B-52 has been the U.S.A.'s main bomber since the 1960s.

engine technology from the British, and swept-wing technology from the Germans, to create a new generation of airborne machines. The resulting American and Russian fighters first faced off over Korea on November 7, 1950, when an American F-80 shot down a Russian MiG-15. Although aircraft performance was comparable on both sides during the Korean War, American pilots were more successful thanks to their superior training.

This new generation of aircraft introduced a new problem—the "sound barrier." Flying at almost Mach 1 (the speed of sound, approximately 700 m.p.h.) could cause an aircraft to become uncontrollable, and even disintegrate. On October 14, 1947, Chuck Yeager overcame this obstacle by flying the experimental X-1 (see page 34) to a speed of Mach 1.06—the first supersonic flight.

Immediately after World War II, most of the world's airlines started to put war surplus DC-3s to commercial use. At the same time, manufacturers began using technology developed during the war to make larger and longer-range airliners such as the Lockheed Constellation and Douglas DC-6, which were able to accommodate over 80 passengers and fly nonstop across the Atlantic Ocean. England was the first country to introduce a jet-powered airliner, the deHavilland Comet in 1952. Although years ahead of its competition in the United States, the Comet lost credibility after experiencing several crashes, allowing the American-made Boeing 707 and Douglas

Aviation Time Line *(continued)*

1953
(May 18) First supersonic flight by a woman, by Jacqueline Cochran flying an F-86

1957
(Oct. 4) First satellite, Sputnik, launched from the Soviet Union

1961
(Apr. 12) First human in space, Soviet cosmonaut Yuri Gagarin

1963
(June 16) First woman in space, Soviet cosmonaut Valentina Tereshkova

1967
(Oct. 3) Fastest flight of an aircraft, by William Knight flying an X-15 to 4,530 m.p.h., U.S.A.

1969
(Feb. 9) First flight of the Boeing 747, U.S.A.

DC-8 to become the jet airliners of choice by 1960.

Bombers, in fact, made the transition to jet power before airliners. The massive B-36, introduced in 1946, boasted four jet as well as six propeller engines, and was followed the next year by the first all-jet bomber, the Boeing B-47. Although over 100 m.p.h. faster than the B-36, it lacked the range necessary to replace its predecessor. The B-52, which first flew in 1954, combined both speed and range—a winning formula that has earned it a key continuing role in America's airborne defense. The long-range jet bombers developed by both England and the Soviet Union during this same period, meanwhile, have been replaced by nuclear missiles. The United States has developed experimental supersonic bombers like the XB-70, which was capable of Mach 3 speeds. But it proved too expensive, and too vulnerable to enemy defenses, to justify putting it into production.

McDonnell Douglas F-4 Phantom II

F-100 Super Saber to the F-106 Delta Dart. In the Soviet Union, jet fighters evolved from the MiG-15 to the Mach 2–capable MiG-21. During the Vietnam War, the fighter of choice for the Americans was the McDonnell Douglas F-4 Phantom II, known for its ruggedness, speed, and ability to carry a large weapon load, but not for its agility. This shortcoming was addressed in the 1970s with the introduction of the F-14, F-15 (see page 46), F-16, and F-18, which combined speed with maneuverability. The Soviets unveiled the Mach 3 MiG-25 and the more versatile MiG-23/27 during this period, but the agility of the American planes would remain unrivaled until the appearance, in the 1980s, of the MiG-29 and Su-27.

Currently in service around the world, the MiG 29 is one of the most advanced Russian fighters.

The last twenty years have seen the introduction of the B-1 bomber and the B-2 "stealth" bomber, though only in limited numbers.

Between the Korean War in the 1950s and the Vietnam War in the 1960s, fighter aircraft grew rapidly in speed, size, and power. In the United States, these fighters become known as the Century series, ranging from the

1969
(July 21) First person to step on the moon, U.S. astronaut Neil Armstrong

1981
(Apr. 12–14) First space shuttle flight

1985
(May 21) Longest flight of a paper aircraft indoors by Tony Feltch, U.S.A.

1986
(Dec. 14–23) First nonstop flight around the world, Dick Rutan and Jeana Yeager (shown at right)

1997
(Sept. 7) First flight by the Lockheed F-22 Raptor

1998
(Oct. 8) Longest duration of flight by a paper aircraft indoors, 27.6 seconds, by Ken Blackburn

What About Space Flight?

Although the Chinese developed the first rockets eight hundred years ago, the development of rockets for space flight did not begin until the 1930s. At that time, Robert Goddard in the United States, Wernher von Braun in Germany, and Sergei Korolev in the Soviet Union all pioneered liquid-fueled rockets. After World War II, the race began in earnest, with Korolev's team the first to orbit a satellite (*Sputnik,* on October 4, 1957),

Goddard

and von Braun's team, now working in the States, following suit on February 1, 1958. Korolev's team was also credited with getting the first man into space, in 1961, with the United States hard on their heels later that same year. It took another eight years to get a man on the moon, America being the only country to have done so to date. Space exploration has also sent unmanned probes to all the planets in the solar system except Pluto. The Soviet Union led the way in the use of space stations, while the United

The Apollo 11 Lunar Module Eagle

States pioneered the reusable space shuttle (see page 58). Today the United States, Russia, and many other nations are joining forces to construct the International Space Station.

European fighters of this time such as the Panavia Tornado, the French Mirage, and the Saab Viggen followed the same trends. The Lockheed F-22 Raptor, which made its maiden flight in 1997, combines speed, maneuverability, and stealth technology, representing the next generation of fighter aircraft.

PLANES FOR TRAVEL AND FUN

Commercial airliners underwent huge changes during the late 1960s and early '70s. The year 1969 saw the introduction of the world's first wide-body jet, the Boeing 747 (see page 38), as well as the maiden flight of the supersonic Concorde (see page 42). One proved much more influential than the other: Although few supersonic jets have been built, wide-body carriers have become extremely popular. They include the Douglas DC-10 and Lockheed L-1011, both introduced in 1970, and the European Airbus A-300, which first flew in 1972. The efficient configuration of the A-300—two wing-mounted engines—has been adopted by the majority of airliners developed since then. A new generation of airliners is currently in development, with the Airbus A380 and the Boeing 747X, each capable of carrying more than 650 passengers, approximately scheduled to arrive in 2005.

Today there are many different forms of recreational flight. The most popular and least expensive options—paragliders, hang gliders, and ultralights (powered hang gliders)—do not even require a

---

Famous Pilots

Byrd, Richard	**Coleman, Bessie**		**Gagarin, Yuri**	**Knight, William**	**Lilienthal, Otto**	
(1888–1957)	*(1896–1926)*		*(1934–1968)*	*(1929–)*	*(1848–1896)*	
First man to fly over North (1926) and South (1929) Poles	*First African-American woman pilot (1921)*	 *Gagarin*	*First man in space (1961)*	*Set flight speed record in the X-15 (4,530 m.p.h.) (1967)*	*German glider pioneer*	*Lilienthal*

The Beaver RX550 light recreational aircraft comes in a kit, weighs 430 pounds, and takes about 200 hours to build.

government license. Many people master these aircraft as the first step toward becoming a licensed pilot, at which point they can either rent a plane, construct a "home-built" (a one-to-six-passenger aircraft made from a kit), or purchase a production airplane of their own, such as a Cessna 172 (see page 50). As well as getting involved in aerobatics or air racing, licensed pilots can also experiment with sailplanes (gliders) or balloons. The possibilities are endless.

Technological advances will continue to allow aircraft to evolve. New composite and ceramic materials will enable lighter structures and the ability to withstand the temperatures of hypersonic flight. Engines of the future will be quieter, more fuel-efficient, and more environmentally friendly, and will operate at higher speeds. In the twenty-first century, these technologies could produce an airliner capable of flying anywhere in the world in under two hours. No doubt the greatest factors in the future of flight, however, will be the same creativity and determination that have led us to where we are today. Thanks to our infinite powers of imagination, the sky is truly the limit.

Quimby, Harriet
(1875–1912)
First licensed woman pilot (1911), first woman to fly across English Channel (1912)

Harriet Quimby

de Rozier, François Pilatre
(1754–1785)
First balloon pilot (1783)

Tuskegee Airmen

Tuskegee Airmen
First African-American fighter squadron (1941)

Wright, Orville
(1871–1948) &
Wilbur
(1867–1912)
First powered airplane flights in history (1903)

Yeager, Jeana
(1952–)
Copilot of first non-stop around-the-world flight (1986)

The Wright Flyer, *which flew tail first, was constructed of spruce and ash covered with muslin.*

Wright *Flyer*

The Wright *Flyer* was the first true airplane. It was designed, built, and flown by Orville and Wilbur Wright, brothers from Dayton, Ohio. When they were kids, their father gave them a rubber-band–powered toy helicopter, and from that moment they were hooked on the idea of flight.

In 1892, the Wrights opened a bicycle shop and began to devote their spare time to learning everything they could about flying. Several people had already been able to create gliders capable of short downhill flights, but no one had successfully added an engine to create a true airplane. The brothers realized that the toughest challenge was to figure out how to control an aircraft— how to make it climb, descend, and turn in response to the pilot's commands.

In July 1899, the Wrights began experimenting with a kite they had built. Although not large enough to carry a pilot, the kite allowed the brothers to develop the canard (see box), which was used to raise and lower the nose of the airplane, and the system of

Wilbur Wright

Orville Wright

Wright Brothers testing a glider at Kitty Hawk

What Is a Canard?

AASI Jetcruzer 500

Canard is the French word for "duck"—which, apparently, is what the French were reminded of when they caught their first glimpse of the Wright brothers' airplane, with its small wing in the front. The word has been used ever since to describe a small wing in the front of a plane, as well as airplanes that fly stabilizer first. The Wrights put the horizontal tail in the front to make the airplane safer, having learned that it would help keep the main wings from stalling. Over the years, most airplanes have adopted the now-traditional tail location at the back of the plane, for reasons that include better weight distribution and the ability to use wing flaps. But there are still some airplanes being made, including the Euro Fighter and the Jetcruzer 500, that use the canard layout.

"wing warping," which lowers one wing while raising the other in order to control turns. In 1900, the Wrights created their first glider and began to look for a good place to fly it—ideally, a site with steady winds, hills from which to launch their creations, and soft sand for safe landings. They found all these elements at Kitty Hawk, North Carolina, where they set up their testing camp. After their 1900 glider proved too small, they returned the following year with a larger, improved model. Although they had created a better flying machine than anyone before them, they knew they had a long way to go to create a reliable and controllable craft. With typical enterprise, they built a wind tunnel in order to gather information on wing shapes, which resulted in longer wings for their 1902 glider. The brothers also added a movable rudder to better execute turns, and they made more than a thousand flights off the hills of Kitty Hawk that year. They were now satisfied they had a consistently controllable glider that was ready for the addition of an engine.

Since no suitable, lightweight engines or propellers existed, the brothers studied existing boat propellers and automobile engines and then used what they learned to design and build an engine for their new airplane. In December 1903, they assembled their first powered aircraft, aptly named the *Flyer,* on the sands of Kitty Hawk.

On December 14, 1903, Wilbur won the coin toss to determine who would pilot the first attempt at powered flight. The *Flyer* moved forward but, instead of taking off, came to an abrupt stop in the sand, and had to be carried back to the hangar for minor repairs. The day of December 17 dawned with a strong but steady wind the Wrights knew would help get the *Flyer* aloft. This time, it was Orville's turn to pilot the plane, and as he became airborne, a camera captured the world's first takeoff. The flight lasted just twelve seconds and covered only 120 feet (about

SPECS

Length:	21 ft. 1 in.
Height:	8 ft. 0 in.
Wingspan:	40 ft. 4 in.
Engine:	One Wright 12 h.p.
Flying Weight:	750 lb.
Max. Speed:	30 m.p.h.
Range:	982 ft.
Max. Altitude:	14 ft.

half the length of a 747), but the era of powered aviation had begun. Wilbur flew next for 175 feet, then Orville piloted the third flight, which spanned 180 feet. The fourth flight saw Wilbur stay aloft for fifty-nine seconds, covering a distance of 852 feet. The Wrights had achieved their goal.

Unfortunately the *Flyer* would never take off again. After the fourth flight, the wind caught the plane, sending it tumbling across the ground. The Wrights disassembled their broken craft and headed back to Dayton, where they continued to design planes that improved on the original *Flyer.* Although much of the world instantly recognized their monumental feat, many people could not believe that two bicycle mechanics had succeeded where top scientists had failed. Today, in recognition of the phenomenal achievement of the two brothers, the *Flyer* hangs prominently in the center of the Smithsonian National Air and Space Museum in Washington, D.C.

WRIGHT *FLYER*

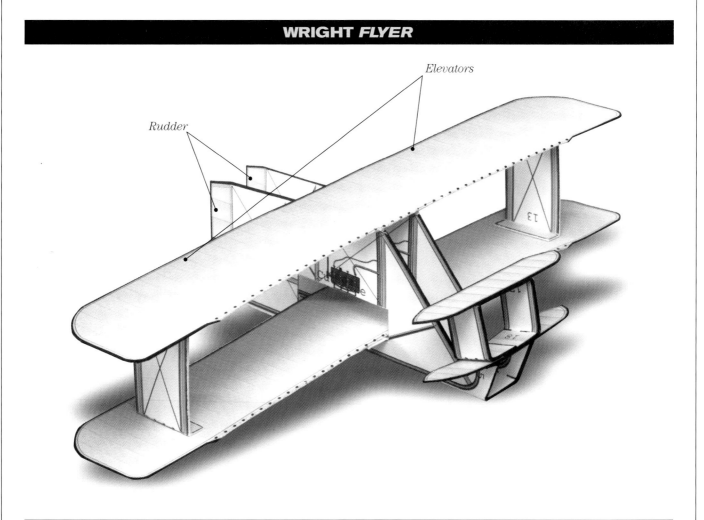

Elevators

Rudder

FLYING TIPS: Before flying, make sure wings are flat and even, not warped. The plane flies best with a gentle toss angled downward. **If your plane dives:** Bend the elevators up a bit or throw the plane a little faster. **If your plane climbs, slows, then dives:** Bend the elevators down a little or throw the plane a little slower. If that doesn't help, try slipping a paper clip over the nose. **If your plane veers:** Bend the rudder a little in the opposite direction of the unwanted turn (i.e., if your plane veers right, bend the rudder left, and vice versa). **Note:** The real Wright *Flyer* used the canard as the elevator; however, your paper replica flies best using the elevator shown.

Cut along heavy solid lines. Score, then fold in along dashed lines (so they're no longer visible); fold away along dotted lines. Glue like letter to like letter. For details, see page 62.

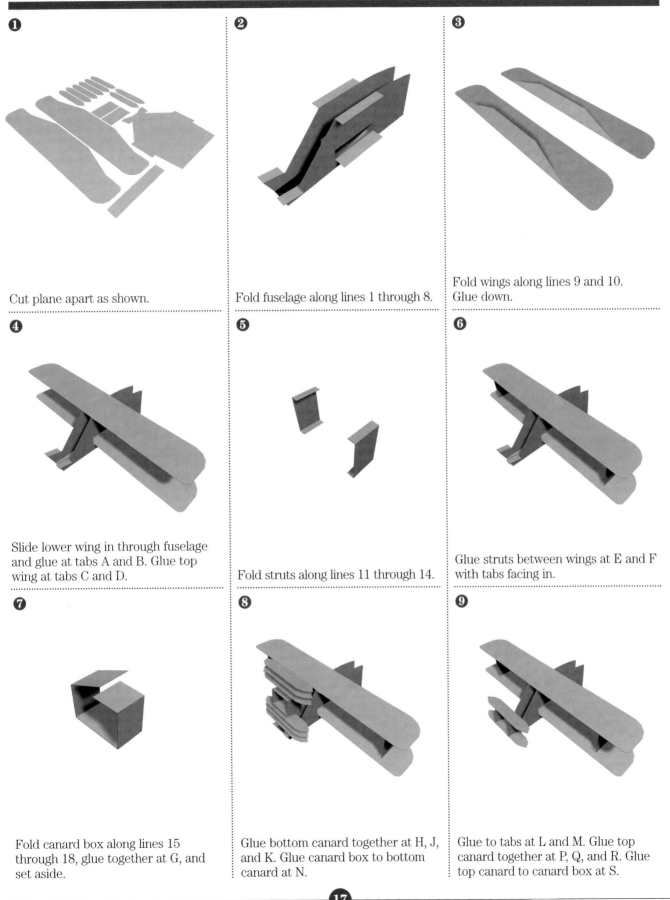

❶ Cut plane apart as shown.

❷ Fold fuselage along lines 1 through 8.

❸ Fold wings along lines 9 and 10. Glue down.

❹ Slide lower wing in through fuselage and glue at tabs A and B. Glue top wing at tabs C and D.

❺ Fold struts along lines 11 through 14.

❻ Glue struts between wings at E and F with tabs facing in.

❼ Fold canard box along lines 15 through 18, glue together at G, and set aside.

❽ Glue bottom canard together at H, J, and K. Glue canard box to bottom canard at N.

❾ Glue to tabs at L and M. Glue top canard together at P, Q, and R. Glue top canard to canard box at S.

Fokker Dr.I Triplane

The Fokker Dr.I triplane is the most recognized of all the planes used in World War I, largely thanks to its association with the legendary Baron Manfred von Richthofen, the "Red Baron." It entered service in August 1917 and was one of the German Air Force's main fighters for the remainder of the conflict.

The Dr.I was developed in the middle of the war, a time of rapid, dramatic advances in aircraft technology and design. When the conflict began, in 1914, there was no such thing as a fighter or a bomber; airplanes were used purely for reconnaissance, and enemy aircraft would simply fly past each other. Soon, however, pilots began to carry handguns with them, a development that saw its logical conclusion with Germany's introduction, in 1915, of the first true

A Sopwith biplane, similar to that used to shoot down the infamous Red Baron

fighter, the Fokker Eindecker E.III. For six months the Fokker Eindecker ruled the skies almost unchallenged, a phenomenon known as the "Fokker scourge." Then, in 1916, the Allies retaliated by introducing new, faster, and more powerful fighter aircraft

The Red Baron, Manfred von Richthofen

such as the French Nieuport and the British Sopwith Pup, rendering the Eindecker nearly obsolete. In fact, aircraft technology was developing so fast that each new model introduced had only six to twelve months before it was eclipsed by a successor. Early 1917 saw the debut of the British Sopwith Triplane, which so impressed the German military with its agility that they sent a request to all their aircraft companies to develop a triplane of their own. The Fokker company, under the direction of chief designer Rheinhold Platz, quickly developed the Dr.I ("Dr" for *Dreidecker,* the German word for "triplane"), which first flew in June 1917 and was introduced into service two months later.

Originally the new aircraft had three wings, but no outboard wing struts or wires—this in an effort to reduce drag and increase speed. Subsequent testing, though, led to a thinner wing shape that required struts for adequate strength. This extremely agile new plane was capable of turning tightly, and climbing to over 14,000 feet in less than fifteen minutes. The performance of the Dr.I made it the choice of many of Germany's top fighter pilots, including Baron von Richthofen.

Von Richthofen was the leading ace of World War I, having shot down eighty enemy fighters and become the leader of the elite German fighter

Restored Dr.I planes are in good flying condition even today.

squadron, the JG.I "circus." The squadron was filled with experienced pilots so confident in their skills that, instead of trying to camouflage their planes, they painted them bright colors. (Von Richthofen's nickname derived from his own plane's bright red color scheme.) But on April 21, 1918, von Richthofen met his match over Sailly-le-Sec in the most famous air battle, or "dogfight," of World War I. Canadian Captain Roy Brown of the RAF, in a Sopwith Camel, was able to finally shoot down the dreaded Red Baron in his Dr.I.

SPECS

Length:	18 ft. 11 in.
Height:	9 ft. 8 in.
Wingspan:	23 ft. 8 in.
Engine:	One 110 h.p. Oberursal rotary
Max. Weight:	1,300 lb.
Max. Speed:	103 m.p.h.
Range:	130 mi.
Max. Altitude:	20,000 ft.

After von Richthofen's death, the JG.I squadron, now under the leadership of Hermann Goering, began switching to the superior Fokker D.VII. This new generation of fighters was faster, better at high altitude, and just as maneuverable as the Dr.Is, which were moved away from the Western Front and relegated to home-defense squadrons. Nonetheless, in addition to being remembered as the airplane of the Red Baron, the Dr.I has earned its place in history as one of the best fighters of its time.

One, Two, or Three Wings—Which Is Best?

Why do old planes have two (biplane) or three (triplane) wings, while modern planes have only one (monoplane)? In the early years of aviation, engines were heavy and not very powerful, making it important for planes to be as light as possible. This resulted in relatively flimsy wings supported by wires and struts, which weighed less than solidly built, unsupported wings. Triplanes were the configuration of choice for a time,

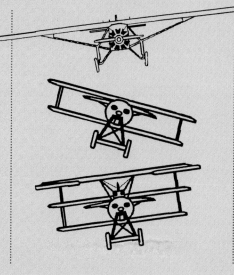

because they allowed a reduced wingspan that increased maneuverability. The drawback was that the extra wing and struts added drag, whereas biplanes offered a better overall balance of strength, speed, and agility. As engines became more powerful and lighter after World War I, minimizing drag to increase speed became more important than reducing weight, leading to the dominance of the monoplane.

FOKKER DR.I TRIPLANE

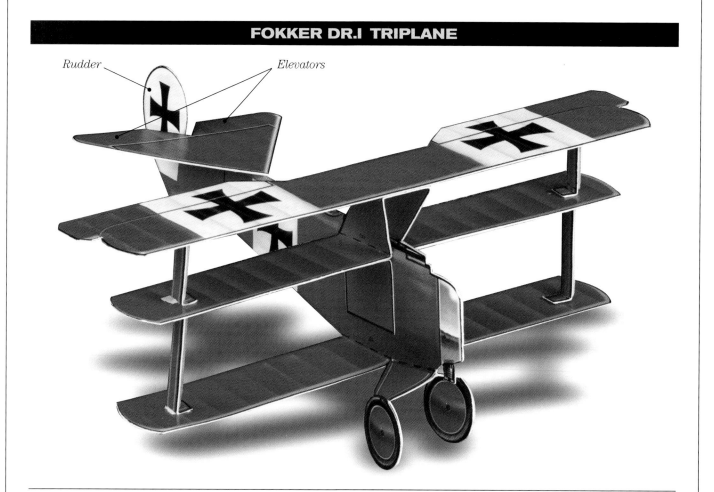

Rudder *Elevators*

FLYING TIPS: Before flying, make sure wings are flat and even, not warped. Then bend the entire front edge of the bottom wing gently downward. The plane flies best with a gentle toss angled downward. **If your plane dives:** Bend the elevators up a bit or throw the plane a little faster. **If your plane climbs, slows, then dives:** Bend the elevators down a little or throw the plane a little slower. If that doesn't help, try slipping a paper clip over the nose. **If your plane veers:** Bend the rudder a little in the opposite direction of the unwanted turn (i.e., if your plane veers right, bend the rudder left, and vice versa).

Cut along heavy solid lines. Score, then fold in along dashed lines (so they're no longer visible); fold away along dotted lines. Glue like letter to like letter. For details, see page 62.

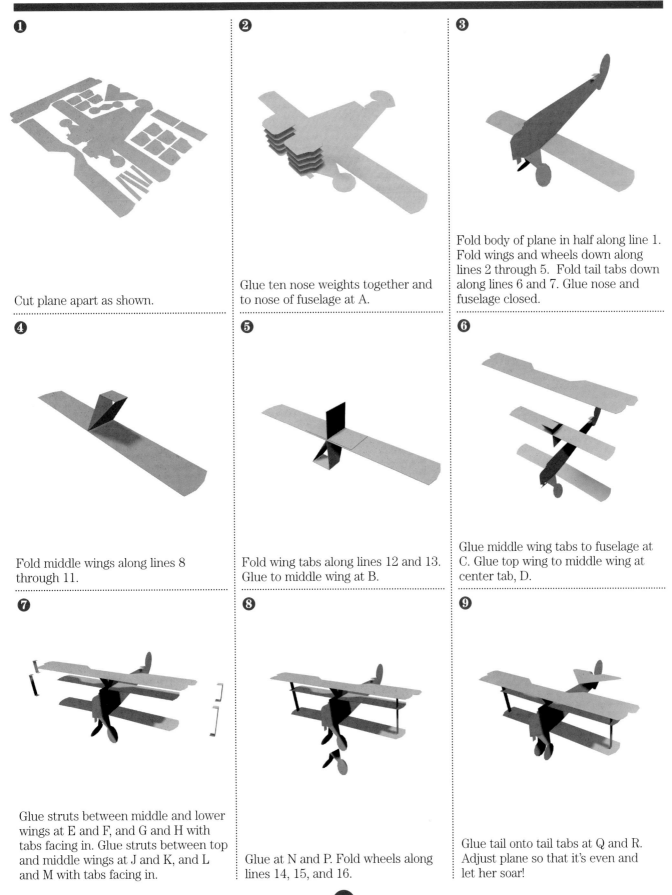

❶

Cut plane apart as shown.

❷

Glue ten nose weights together and to nose of fuselage at A.

❸

Fold body of plane in half along line 1. Fold wings and wheels down along lines 2 through 5. Fold tail tabs down along lines 6 and 7. Glue nose and fuselage closed.

❹

Fold middle wings along lines 8 through 11.

❺

Fold wing tabs along lines 12 and 13. Glue to middle wing at B.

❻

Glue middle wing tabs to fuselage at C. Glue top wing to middle wing at center tab, D.

❼

Glue struts between middle and lower wings at E and F, and G and H with tabs facing in. Glue struts between top and middle wings at J and K, and L and M with tabs facing in.

❽

Glue at N and P. Fold wheels along lines 14, 15, and 16.

❾

Glue tail onto tail tabs at Q and R. Adjust plane so that it's even and let her soar!

Ryan NYP–
Spirit of St. Louis

Lindbergh was nicknamed "Lucky Lindy" and the "Lone Eagle" by the press.

On May 21, 1927, the *Spirit of St. Louis*, piloted by Charles Lindbergh, became the first airplane to fly nonstop from New York to Paris. Lindbergh's remarkable feat is deemed by many to be the greatest in the history of flight, and is credited as paving the way for commercial aviation by demonstrating the safety of air travel.

In 1926 Charles Lindbergh was a twenty-four-year-old pilot flying mail between St. Louis and Chicago. He had heard about the $25,000 Orteig Prize for the first New York–to–Paris flight and believed he could win it. Soon after sharing his plans with the well-connected flight students he was teaching in St. Louis, he had raised the money to have an airplane designed and built specifically for the trip. After being turned down by a string of manufacturers, he successfully persuaded the small Ryan Airlines Company in San Diego to take on the project. Work started in late February 1927, with everyone at the company toiling alongside Lindbergh, virtually around the clock, to get the new plane designed and built. Meanwhile, a series of would-be prizewinners tried, and failed, to complete the flight. The new craft was a modified version of the Ryan M-2 mail plane, and was designated the Ryan NYP, which stood for the intended route from New York to Paris. The NYP was christened the *Spirit of St. Louis* in order to promote the city where its financial backers lived. While the other competitors were relying on multiple engines and several pilots to endure the 3,600-mile trip, the *Spirit of St. Louis* used a single engine, the reliable new Wright Whirlwind. Lindbergh knew that his best chance of winning was with one good engine and one good pilot.

SPECS
Length: 27 ft. 7 in.
Height: 9 ft. 10 in.
Wingspan: 46 ft. 0 in.
Engine: One 237 h.p. Wright J-5C Whirlwind
Max. Weight: 5,100 lb.
Max. Speed: 130 m.p.h.
Range: 4,350 mi.
Max. Altitude: Unknown

On April 28, 1927, just two months after starting the project, Lindbergh flew the *Spirit of St. Louis* for the first time. Although it had low stability, it performed very well, and he was confident it was the right plane for the long trip. After a quick series of test flights, Lindbergh took off from San Diego on May 10, flying nonstop to St. Louis and then, a few hours later, direct to New York City. Several other competitors were also preparing to depart, and Lindbergh was determined to beat them.

The morning of May 20, 1927, was damp and cloudy. Lindbergh knew from the weather reports

First Flight Across the Atlantic?

Contrary to popular belief, Lindbergh was not the first person to fly across the Atlantic Ocean. In May 1919 the U.S. Navy seaplane NC-4 crossed the Atlantic, refueling twice at sea from waiting Navy ships. The first nonstop flight came only a month later, when John Alcock and Arthur Whitten Brown flew 1,890 miles from Canada to Ireland in a converted World War I bomber. Lindbergh's flight was the first *solo* crossing, and followed a route almost twice as long as the shortest distance across the ocean.

Lindbergh had to use a periscope to see around the fuel tanks at the front of the plane.

that if he could get his plane airborne, the trip across the Atlantic was feasible. He lined up on the grass runway of Roosevelt Airfield, Long Island, and gave the NYP full throttle. The combination of the heavy fuel load and muddy ground made the takeoff slow and uncertain, but the plane finally broke free of the ground and cleared the power lines at the end of the runway—by a mere twenty feet! By nightfall, Lindbergh had passed the coast of Newfoundland and now had to find his way over 2,000 miles of open ocean while also battling fatigue. (He had not been able to sleep the night before the flight.) By midafternoon of the next day, he saw fishing boats, and then land. After sixteen hours over open ocean, guided only by a compass and the stars, Lindbergh crossed the coast of Ireland only a few miles off his intended course. Six hours later, thirty-three hours and 3,600 miles after takeoff, Lindbergh landed at Le Bourget Field in Paris in front of a waiting crowd of 100,000.

Lindbergh returned to the United States a hero, honored by parades and cheering crowds in both Washington, D.C., and New York City. From July 1927 to April 1928, he made a flying tour of the United States, Central, and South America. At the end of the tour, Lindbergh (the only person ever to pilot the *Spirit of St. Louis*) flew to Washington, D.C., to present the plane to the Smithsonian Institution, where it has been on display to this day. Lindbergh's flight demonstrated the dramatic improvements that aircraft had made in performance and reliability, and his charm and enthusiasm captured the imagination of the world. He single-handedly changed the public's perception of aviation and ushered in a new era of air transportation.

RYAN NYP–*SPIRIT OF ST. LOUIS*

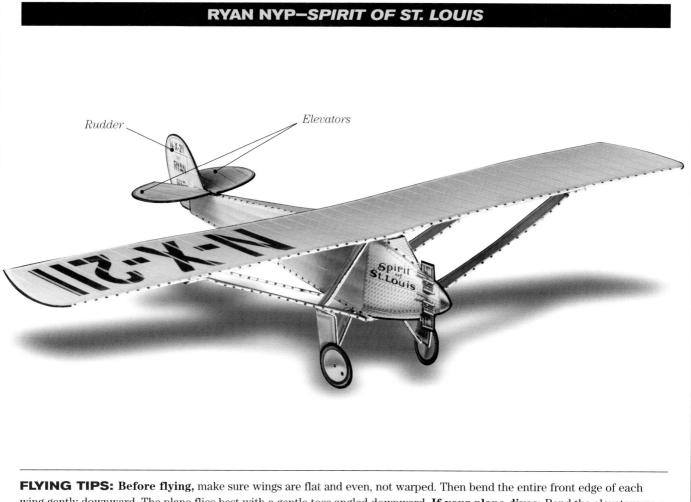

Rudder   *Elevators*

FLYING TIPS: Before flying, make sure wings are flat and even, not warped. Then bend the entire front edge of each wing gently downward. The plane flies best with a gentle toss angled downward. **If your plane dives:** Bend the elevators up a bit or throw the plane a little faster. **If your plane climbs, slows, then dives:** Bend the elevators down a bit or throw the plane a little slower. If that doesn't help, try slipping a paper clip over the nose. **If your plane veers:** Bend the rudder a little in the opposite direction of the unwanted turn (i.e., if your plane veers right, bend the rudder left, and vice versa).

Cut along heavy solid lines. Score, then fold in along dashed lines (so they're no longer visible); fold away along dotted lines. Glue like letter to like letter. For details, see page 62.

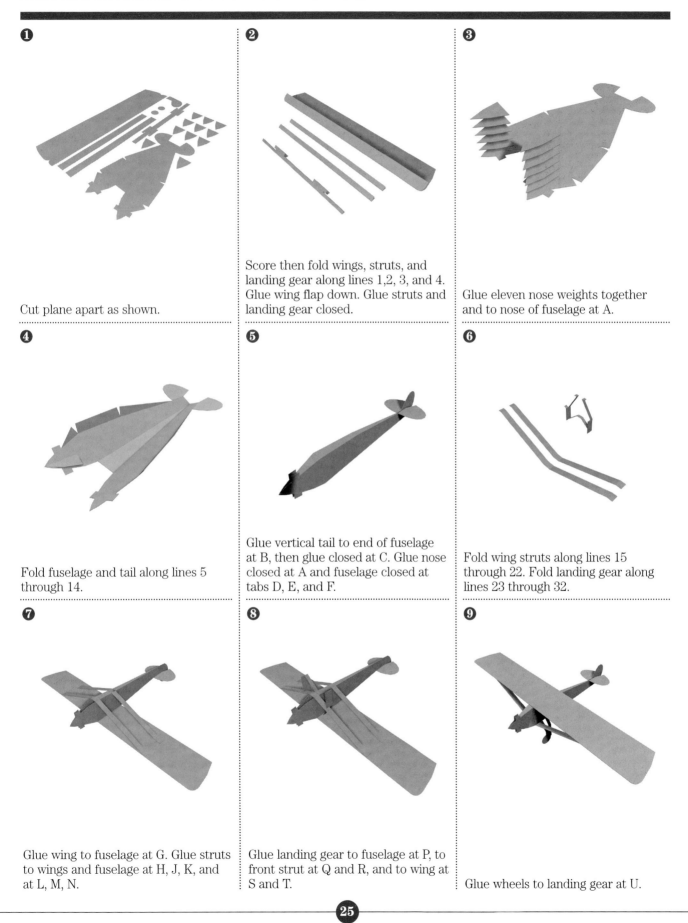

❶

Cut plane apart as shown.

❷

Score then fold wings, struts, and landing gear along lines 1,2, 3, and 4. Glue wing flap down. Glue struts and landing gear closed.

❸

Glue eleven nose weights together and to nose of fuselage at A.

❹

Fold fuselage and tail along lines 5 through 14.

❺

Glue vertical tail to end of fuselage at B, then glue closed at C. Glue nose closed at A and fuselage closed at tabs D, E, and F.

❻

Fold wing struts along lines 15 through 22. Fold landing gear along lines 23 through 32.

❼

Glue wing to fuselage at G. Glue struts to wings and fuselage at H, J, K, and at L, M, N.

❽

Glue landing gear to fuselage at P, to front strut at Q and R, and to wing at S and T.

❾

Glue wheels to landing gear at U.

Douglas DC-3

The DC-3 revolutionized both commercial air travel and military cargo airlift, introducing new standards of airline capacity, performance, and reliability. Even today, sixty-five years after the first model was introduced, DC-3s are still in service around the world.

In the early 1930s, airline travel was in its infancy, and airlines still remained dependent on transporting mail to make a profit. In 1933, after Boeing unveiled the innovative Model 247 airliner, Douglas Aircraft responded with the introduction of the DC-1. An improved model, the DC-2, followed soon after. In 1935, American Airlines asked Douglas to enlarge the fuselage of the DC-2 to allow room for sleeper berths, and on December 17, 1935, the DC-3 Douglas Sleeper Transport made its first flight.

Although the DC-3 resembled its predecessors, it was fundamentally superior. Whereas the Boeing 247 carried 10 passengers and the DC-2 carried 14, the DC-3 could carry 21. It was as fast as any other airliner, could fly farther, and quickly developed a reputation for durability. Airlines began to order the new model in droves,

This 1925 Supermarine S.4 was clocked at 226 m.p.h.

What Happened to Seaplanes?

Prior to World War II, many of the largest transport aircraft were seaplanes, since there were few runways large enough to accommodate planes of their size. These pontooned planes carried mail and passengers between major cities, landing on their harbors. The tremendous number of large runways constructed during the war, however, enabled seaplanes to be replaced by their more efficient wheeled counterparts.

and by 1939, DC-3s accounted for 90 percent of the world's airline traffic (95 percent in the United States).

When World War II broke out, the military realized that the same qualities that made the DC-3 the world's most popular airliner would also make it a superb troop carrier and cargo aircraft. The military version was designated the C-47 (also C-53, C-117, and R4D) and quickly went into mass production, reaching a peak of one every thirty minutes. The C-47 was so central to the war effort that General Eisenhower designated it one of the four most important weapons of the conflict. After the war, the C-47 took part in the Berlin Airlift, carried troops and supplies in the Korean War, and was even used in Vietnam as a gunship (a cargo aircraft armed with artillery). Although no longer used by the U.S. military, C-47s are still deployed by other air forces around the world.

After World War II, a large number of military C-47s became surplus, and were purchased by most of the world's airlines. Some had seating for up to 36 passengers, but the majority

The DC-3 was dubbed "Gooney Bird" by American pilots in World War II because, like its seabird namesake, it was clumsy on the ground but graceful in the air.

seated 21 to 28. Many others were used to fly cargo or mail. Though most were eventually replaced by more modern aircraft, the DC-3 is so strong, reliable, and fundamentally well designed that many have been upgraded and remain in service today. Several engine replacements have been implemented, some using a turboprop, or jet-powered propeller.

In 1949, Douglas introduced the Super DC-3 modification program, which took existing models and replaced the outer wings, lengthened the fuselage, and added more powerful engines. DC3s are so durable that some have clocked more than six years of flight time in the air.

The DC-3 ushered in the modern era of airline travel, and was also acclaimed as the most important aircraft the Allies possessed in the Second World War. When production ceased in 1947, over 13,000 had been built; amazingly, 3,000 of them are still in operation around the globe.

SPECS

Length:	64 ft. 6 in.
Height:	16 ft. 11 in.
Wingspan:	95 ft. 0 in.
Engines:	Two 1200 h.p. Wright R-1830-92
Max. Weight:	25,200 lb.
Max. Speed:	230 m.p.h.
Range:	1,500 mi.
Max. Altitude:	23,000 ft.

Tail Wheel vs. Nose Wheel

In the 1940s and '50s, most new airplanes went from having a tail landing wheel to a wheel in the nose. The main advantage of the tail wheel was its light weight and suitability for rough airstrips. During and after World War II, however, many smooth, hard-surface airfields were built, reducing the need for rough-field capability. Planes with nose wheels are also easier to land and steer than those with tail wheels.

DOUGLAS DC-3

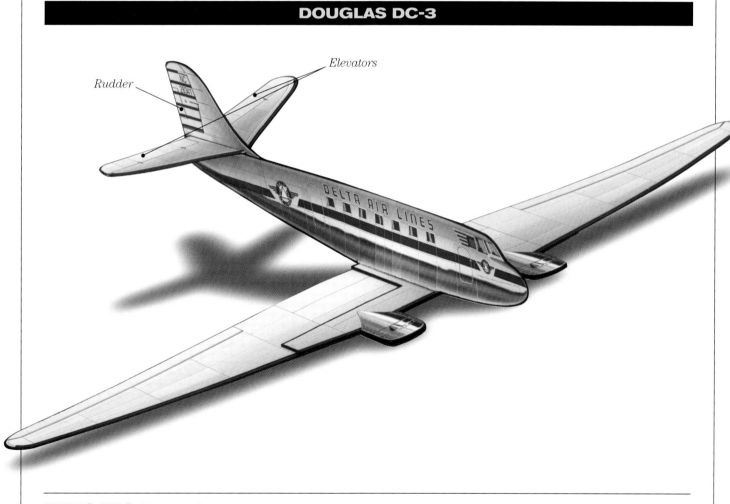

Rudder *Elevators*

FLYING TIPS: Before flying, make sure wings are flat and even, not warped. Then bend the entire front edge of each wing gently downward. The plane flies best with a gentle toss angled downward. **If your plane dives:** Bend the elevators up a bit or throw the plane a little faster. **If your plane climbs, slows, then dives:** Bend the elevators down a bit or throw the plane a little slower. If that doesn't help, try slipping a paper clip over the nose. **If your plane veers:** Bend the rudder a little in the opposite direction of the unwanted turn (i.e., if your plane veers right, bend the rudder left, and vice versa).

Cut along heavy solid lines. Score, then fold in along dashed lines (so they're no longer visible); fold away along dotted lines. Glue like letter to like letter. For details, see page 62.

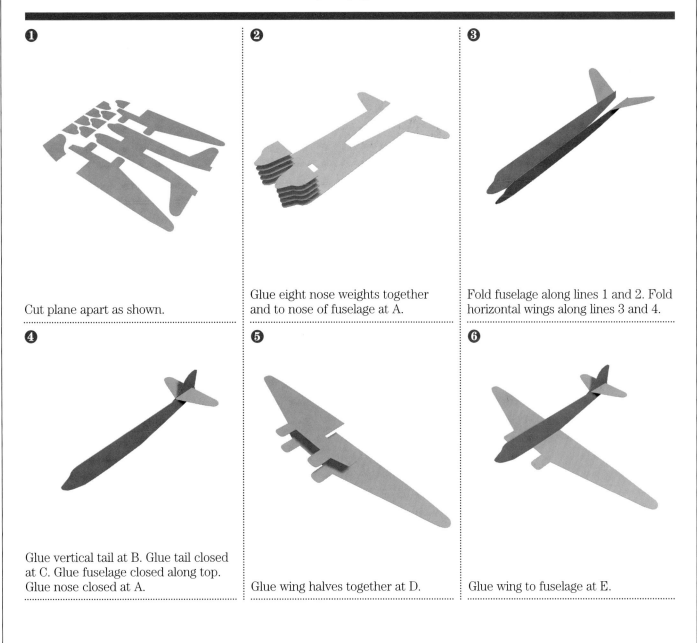

❶ Cut plane apart as shown.

❷ Glue eight nose weights together and to nose of fuselage at A.

❸ Fold fuselage along lines 1 and 2. Fold horizontal wings along lines 3 and 4.

❹ Glue vertical tail at B. Glue tail closed at C. Glue fuselage closed along top. Glue nose closed at A.

❺ Glue wing halves together at D.

❻ Glue wing to fuselage at E.

North American P-51 Mustang

During World War II, Mustangs served in almost every combat zone.

Fast, maneuverable, and with the range to operate deep into enemy territory, the P-51 Mustang is considered one of the greatest fighters of World War II. It was developed at the beginning of the war and created such high demand that, when hostilities ceased in 1945, over 15,000 had been built.

In early 1940, unable to produce enough fighters for the growing war in Europe, the British government decided to purchase some from the United States. Many of the larger American aircraft manu-facturers were already committed to producing fighter planes for the U.S. military, so the British approached North American Aviation, with whom they had an existing contract for the supply of the new Harvard (AT-6) training aircraft. Impressed with the AT-6s, the British proposed that North American—a company that had never made a fighter of its own—produce Curtiss Kittyhawk fighters under license to add to the existing British fleet. North American, however, had been studying how to make an improved fighter, and convinced the British

Chuck Yeager entering a P-51

to let them design a completely new plane. Beating a very tight four-month production deadline, the prototype P-51 Mustang was ready in just 117 days, although the first flight was held up because of a delay in engine delivery.

The P-51 Mustang incorporated many new features. An innovative air scoop brought air into and out of the large radiator so smoothly that it reduced drag on the airplane, and may even have produced extra thrust from the heated air it expelled. The Mustang also boasted a newly invented low-drag wing and fuel tanks with two to three times the capacity of the competition. New features aside, it was a fundamentally well-designed aircraft: light, strong, and responsive.

By the summer of 1942, the British Mustangs were in combat, and received very favorable reviews for every aspect of their performance except one—their limited power at high altitude. Since the United States was interested in the new plane, it investigated the problem and found a solution in the shape of the Rolls-Royce Merlin engine. Several Mustangs were modified by installing the Merlin instead of the original Allison engine, a move that clearly realized the full potential of the aircraft. The new model instantly went into mass production, with the version built in Inglewood, California, designated the P-51B, and an identical version designated

Silver or Green?

Most combat aircraft are painted green or blue so as to blend in with the ground and sky for camouflage purposes. Near the end of World War II, though, Mustangs flew without paint in their natural, shiny aluminum finish. Why? With enemy fighters dwindling and on the defensive, Mustang pilots decided that camouflage was less important than making their planes lighter and faster.

P-51C built in Dallas, Texas. The large fuel tanks, in particular, became essential to the Allies' war strategy: Because of their long range, P-51s could accompany bombers on runs deep inside enemy territory. In 1944, the P-51D added a bubble canopy for improved visibility and a dorsal fin for increased stability. It became the most popular variant, with nearly 8,000 produced.

Unlike most World War II aircraft, the P-51 enjoyed a military career that continued beyond the end of the conflict. Versions of the P-51 remained in service post-1945, and went on to be used in the Korean War. (One version used in Korea even joined two P-51 fuselages with a short center wing; named first the P-82 and

SPECS	
Length: 32 ft. 2 in.	
Height: 13 ft. 8 in.	
Wingspan: 37 ft. 0 in.	
Engine: One 1695 h.p. Rolls-Royce Merlin	
Max. Weight: 11,600 lb.	
Max. Speed: 437 m.p.h.	
Range: 950–2,080 mi.	
Max. Altitude: 41,900 ft.	

Colonel C. E. "Bud" Anderson shot down sixteen enemy aircraft in his P-51 nicknamed Old Crow.

then the F-82, it served as a night fighter.) In addition, many surplus planes were sold to a number of other countries, with Mustangs serving in as many as fifty-five nations.

The Mustang combines all the things that make a great fighter—speed, maneuverability, strength, range, and firepower. Loved by its pilots and those of the bombers it protected, and feared by the enemy, it has earned a highly distinguished position in the history of military aviation.

NORTH AMERICAN P-51 MUSTANG

FLYING TIPS: Before flying, make sure wings are flat and even, not warped. Then bend the entire front edge of each wing gently downward. The plane flies best with a gentle toss angled downward. **If your plane dives:** Bend the elevators up a bit or throw the plane a little faster. **If your plane climbs, slows, then dives:** Bend the elevators down a bit or throw the plane a little slower. If that doesn't help, try slipping a paper clip over the nose. **If your plane veers:** Bend the rudder a little in the opposite direction of the unwanted turn (i.e., if your plane veers right, bend the rudder left, and vice versa).

Cut along heavy solid lines. Score, then fold in along dashed lines (so they're no longer visible); fold away along dotted lines. Glue like letter to like letter. For details, see page 62.

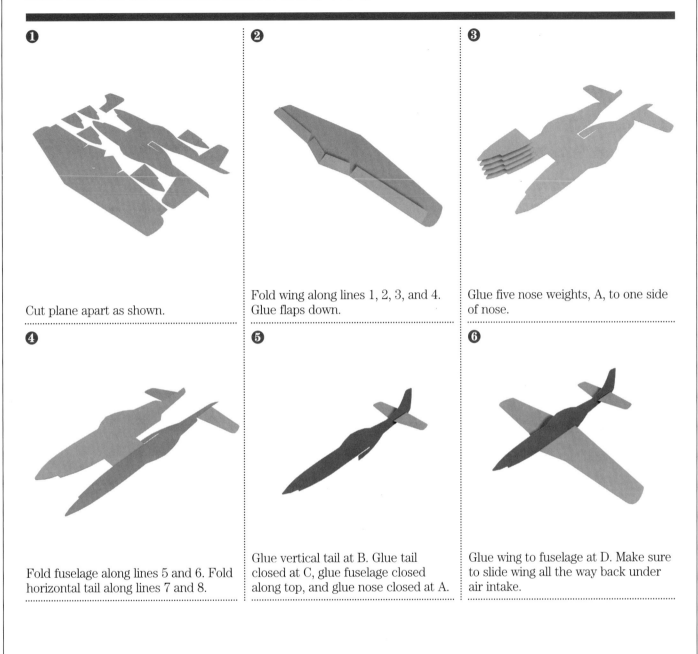

① Cut plane apart as shown.

② Fold wing along lines 1, 2, 3, and 4. Glue flaps down.

③ Glue five nose weights, A, to one side of nose.

④ Fold fuselage along lines 5 and 6. Fold horizontal tail along lines 7 and 8.

⑤ Glue vertical tail at B. Glue tail closed at C, glue fuselage closed along top, and glue nose closed at A.

⑥ Glue wing to fuselage at D. Make sure to slide wing all the way back under air intake.

Bell X-1

Shock waves from an aircraft (similar to the shock waves visible in the exhaust plume above) cause a sudden change of pressure in the eardrum, experienced as a sonic boom.

On October 14, 1947, U.S. Air Force captain Charles "Chuck" Yeager became the first pilot to fly a plane faster than the speed of sound, taking the Bell X-1 to Mach 1.06 (700 m.p.h., 1.06 times the speed of sound). This single flight dispelled the myth that aircraft could not break the sound barrier and ushered in the supersonic era.

During World War II, fighter aircraft had become progressively faster, and in steep dives some approached the speed of sound. During these dives, pilots reported that the aircraft would shake violently, and the control stick would become almost impossible to move, causing the aircraft to become unmanageable. Even when the control stick could be moved, the aircraft would respond erratically. Scientists discovered that flight approaching the speed of sound created shock waves, which in turn created the turbulence that caused the uncontrollability. After the war, the U.S. government initiated test programs to determine a way to overcome this phenomenon, which became known as the "sound barrier" or the "sonic wall." In March 1945, the U.S.

Why Orange?

The X-1 was a very small aircraft and flew very high. It was painted orange to increase its visibility from the ground.

Army Air Force and the National Advisory Committee for Aeronautics (which later became NASA) contracted the Bell Aircraft Corporation to construct a rocket-powered research aircraft. The Army Air Force assigned the plane the designation XS-1 for "Experimental Sonic-1," later shortened to X-1.

Bell Aircraft had an obstacle to overcome. No one had ever designed a supersonic aircraft before, and since no supersonic wind tunnels existed for testing, Bell simply had to do without them. The X-1 was built in Buffalo, New York, and constructed of high-strength aluminum, with propellant tanks made of steel. For maximum power at high altitude, Bell engineers selected a rocket engine built by Reaction Motors, Inc., to power the X-1, and the entire body of the airplane served as a fuel tank, with the ability to carry 5,000 pounds of fuel. The engineers realized that machine-gun bullets could travel at supersonic speeds, so they constructed the nose of the aircraft in the shape of a .50-caliber bullet. In only ten months the X-1 was designed, constructed, and ready for its first flight.

The first X-1 pilot was Chalmers "Slick" Goodlin, a civilian research pilot who was paid risk bonuses for flying the unproven airplane. Flight-testing began on January 25, 1946, with an unpowered glide at Pinecastle Army Air Field in Orlando, Florida. The X-1 was designed to take off under its own power, but in order to conserve as much fuel as possible for high-speed flight, and for safety reasons, the X-1 was air-launched from the bomb bay of a B-29 bomber. Subsequent testing was done in the California desert at Muroc Field, now known as Edwards Air Force Base, with powered flights up to Mach 0.8. The danger of flying at these speeds was proven in September 1946 when *The*

Swallow, a British DH108, was sent up in an attempt to break the sound barrier and broke apart as it approached Mach 1, killing the pilot, Geoffrey deHavilland Jr., who was the son of the man whose company built the DH108. This caused Slick Goodlin to request an additional $150,000 before trying to take the X-1 to supersonic speed. In response, the Air

Chuck Yeager piloted an improved version of the X-1, the X-1A, to Mach 2.4 in 1953.

Force asked its fighter test pilots to volunteer as replacements. Captain Charles "Chuck" Yeager, a P-51 fighter ace eager to take on such an exciting assignment, was selected. He was paid his regular Air Force captain's pay of $283.00 a month. Yeager made his first flight in the X-1 on August 29, 1947, and it was during his ninth flight less than two months later that he became the first pilot to break the sound barrier, traveling at Mach 1.06. Yeager was also the only pilot to take off in the X-1 from the ground, which he accomplished on January 5, 1949.

After breaking through the sonic wall, the X-1 had nowhere else to go but higher, faster, and into history. The highest speed attained by the X-1 was Mach 1.45 (957 m.p.h.) by Yeager on March 26, 1948. The following year, Major Frank Everest Jr.

SPECS

Length: 31 ft.	
Height: 10 ft. 10 in.	
Wingspan: 28 ft.	
Engine: Reaction Motor XLR-11-RM-3, 6000-lb. thrust	
Empty Weight: 7,000 lb.	
Max. Speed: Mach 1.45 (957 m.p.h.)	
Range: Less than 100 mi.	
Max. Altitude: 71,902 ft.	

Yeager nicknamed the X-1 Glamorous Glennis *in honor of his wife.*

piloted the X-1 to its highest altitude of 71,902 feet.

In all, the X-1 completed seventy-eight flights, and on August 26, 1950, the Air Force presented it to the Smithsonian Institution. During the ceremony, Air Force Chief of Staff General Hoyt Vandenberg said, "The X-1 marked the end of the first great period of the air age, and the beginning of the second. In a few moments the subsonic period became history and the supersonic period was born."

The X-1 Fleet

The X-1 was the first of six in the X-1 series. The X-1A was the highest performance version, attaining a speed of Mach 2.435 and an altitude of 90,000 feet; however, it was destroyed when an engine exploded in 1955. Two others were destroyed during ground testing, but the X-1E, which achieved Mach 2, sits on a pedestal at Edwards Air Force Base. The X-1B completed twenty-seven flights for thermal research and is now on display at the Air Force Museum at Wright Patterson Air Force Base in Ohio. In total, the X-1 series completed 156 flights.

BELL X-1

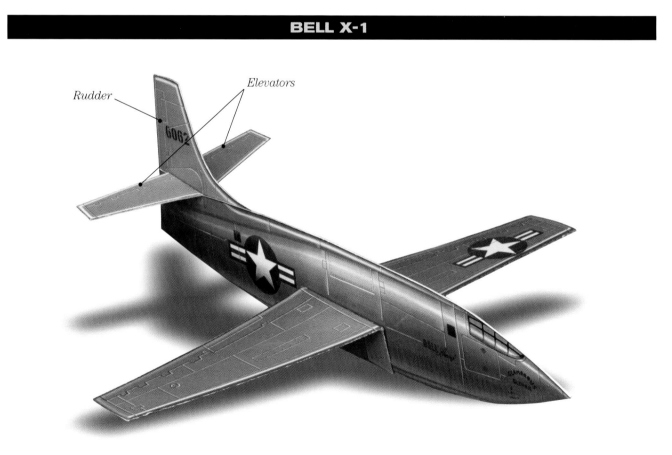

Rudder

Elevators

FLYING TIPS: Before flying, make sure wings are flat and even, not warped. Then bend the entire front edge of each wing gently downward. The plane flies best with a gentle toss angled downward. **If your plane dives:** Bend the elevators up a bit or throw the plane a little faster. **If your plane climbs, slows, then dives:** Bend the elevators down a bit or throw the plane a little slower. **If your plane veers:** Bend the rudder a little in the opposite direction of the unwanted turn (i.e., if your plane veers right, bend the rudder left, and vice versa).

Cut along heavy solid lines. Score, then fold in along dashed lines (so they're no longer visible); fold away along dotted lines. Glue like letter to like letter. For details, see page 62.

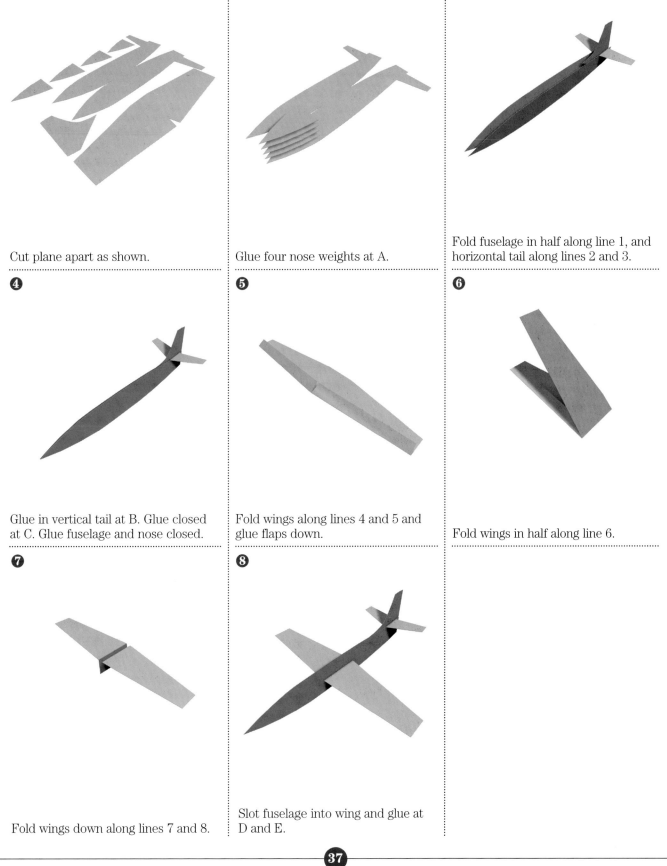

❶
Cut plane apart as shown.

❷
Glue four nose weights at A.

❸
Fold fuselage in half along line 1, and horizontal tail along lines 2 and 3.

❹
Glue in vertical tail at B. Glue closed at C. Glue fuselage and nose closed.

❺
Fold wings along lines 4 and 5 and glue flaps down.

❻
Fold wings in half along line 6.

❼
Fold wings down along lines 7 and 8.

❽
Slot fuselage into wing and glue at D and E.

Boeing 747

The 747 is constructed of approximately six million parts.

Still the largest airliner in the world, the 747 was over twice the size of its nearest competition when it first flew in 1969. The 747 is today, and will forever remain, one of aviation's most outstanding acheivements.

Starting in the 1950s, Boeing sought to replace propeller-driven aircraft with jets to keep up with the world's changing aircraft technology. Boeing's first commercial jetliner was the 707, developed in the late 1950s with the ability to carry 189 passengers across the Atlantic Ocean. For its time the 707 was one of the largest and longest-range passenger airliners in the world. Next came the 720, a smaller, shorter version of the 707 that was introduced in 1959 for domestic flights, followed by the 727 in 1963. Although the same size as the 707 and just as fast, the 727 was made for short flights and short runways. In 1967, Boeing introduced its smallest jet, the 737, which was also geared for domestic flights. By this time, the 707 was in need of updating to keep pace with the competition. In the early 1960s, Boeing had canvassed various airlines about their needs, and all replied that they wanted the increased efficiency and capacity a larger plane would afford. Rather than improve the 707, Boeing decided to produce a radically new airplane, the 747.

Boeing had been studying large-cargo aircraft concepts, and was now able to apply the lessons it had learned to the new airliner. Numerous studies were performed to see if such a huge craft could

747s under construction

new versions of the plane with improved capacity, range, and efficiency have been introduced, with even more variants still planned. Many credit the 747 with introducing the concept of affordable international travel.

This unique aircraft has had several unusual applications. When NASA needed a means of transporting the space shuttle orbiter, a 747 was modified to carry the spacecraft piggyback. Another version, the E-4B, is used as a flying military command center. Two 747s, sharing the role of *Air Force One*, were

747 Trivia

• The 747 fleet has logged 33 billion statute miles—enough to make 69,000 trips to the moon and back.
• The 747 fleet has flown 3.3 billion people—the equivalent of over half the world's population.
• A 747 typically takes off at 180 m.p.h., cruises at 565 m.p.h., and lands at 160 m.p.h.
• For a typical international flight, one 747 operator uses no fewer than 5.5 tons of food supplies and more than 50,000 in-flight service items.

really work, not just in the air but on the ground. New ways were devised to move the expected 500 passengers on and off the plane, including the innovative use of two aisles. A special fifty-foot-tall car was even built to see if pilots could taxi such a monster around airports. Then there was the fact that a plane of this size would require an enormous building in which to construct it—and indeed, the manufacturing plant for the 747 in Everett, Washington, remains the largest building on the planet.

Airlines around the world soon realized that the performance and size of the 747 were ideal for making long international flights, and orders for the gigantic airliner began coming in. Although some versions were built for transporting up to 600 people on short flights, most were built for flying 300 to 500 passengers over several thousand miles. In fact, the record for the most people ever to fly on a single airplane was set by a 1991 evacuation flight from Ethiopia. (The 747 took off with 1,086 passengers, but landed with 1,088—two babies were born in the air.) In the years since its introduction,

modified into suitable airborne digs for the U.S. president. Another variant, currently being built, will house a giant laser in its nose capable of shooting down missiles in mid-flight.

Airbus Industries is planning to build an airliner bigger than the 747, called the A380, that would carry over 650 passengers. In response, Boeing is working on something called the 747X Stretch, with a similar capacity. With over 1,260 built, and new versions still to come, the 747 will be a common sight in the skies around the world for decades to come.

SPECS

Length: 231 ft. 10 in.	
Height: 63 ft. 8 in.	
Wingspan: 211 ft. 5 in.	
Engines: Four Pratt & Whitney PW4062—63,300 lb. thrust each, or Four Rolls-Royce RB211-524H—59,500 lb. thrust each, or Four General Electric CF6-80C2B5F—62,100 lb. thrust each	
Max. Weight: 875,000 lb.	
Cruise Speed: 0.85 Mach (565 m.p.h.)	
Range: 8,430 mi.	
Max. Altitude: 45,000 ft.	

Why the Hump?

Why does the 747 have that distinctive hump on its front? Because it was designed to allow some versions to function as cargo planes with the ability to carry up to 124 tons of material. The cockpit was located on the hump on top of the fuselage so the entire nose could be opened to accommodate large cargo items. On passenger variants, the pilot and copilot sit at the front of the hump and passengers sit in the aft section. Early versions of the 747 had seats for 32 passengers at the top of a spiral staircase. Later versions extended the hump further aft to allow room for 69 passengers, and replaced the spiral staircase with a straight one.

BOEING 747

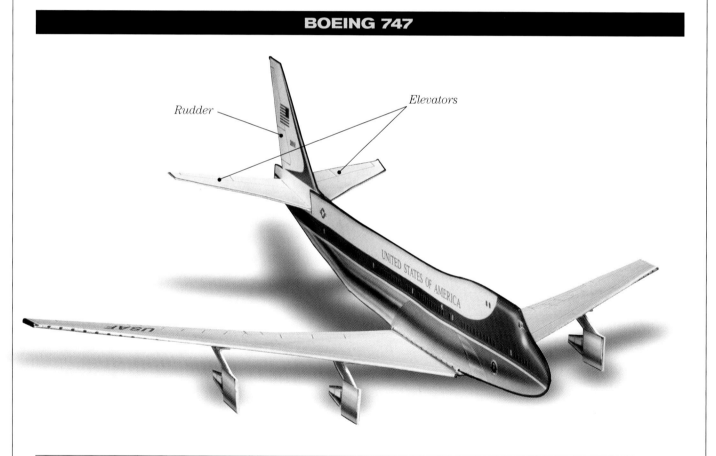

Rudder

Elevators

FLYING TIPS: Before flying, make sure wings are flat and even, not warped. Then bend the entire front edge of each wing gently downward. Add a small paper clip to the nose of the plane. The plane flies best with a gentle toss angled downward. **If your plane dives:** Bend the elevators up a bit or throw the plane a little faster. **If your plane climbs, slows, then dives:** Bend the elevators down a bit or throw the plane a little slower. **If your plane veers:** Bend the rudder a little in the opposite direction of the unwanted turn (i.e., if your plane veers right, bend the rudder left, and vice versa).

Cut along heavy solid lines. Score, then fold in along dashed lines (so they're no longer visible); fold away along dotted lines. Glue like letter to like letter. For details, see page 62.

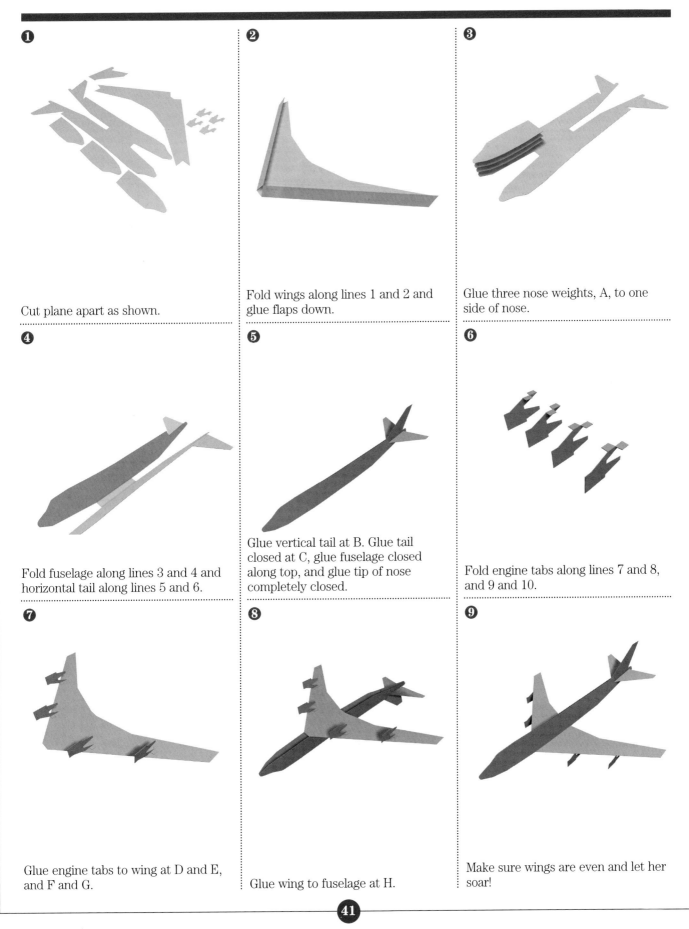

❶ Cut plane apart as shown.

❷ Fold wings along lines 1 and 2 and glue flaps down.

❸ Glue three nose weights, A, to one side of nose.

❹ Fold fuselage along lines 3 and 4 and horizontal tail along lines 5 and 6.

❺ Glue vertical tail at B. Glue tail closed at C, glue fuselage closed along top, and glue tip of nose completely closed.

❻ Fold engine tabs along lines 7 and 8, and 9 and 10.

❼ Glue engine tabs to wing at D and E, and F and G.

❽ Glue wing to fuselage at H.

❾ Make sure wings are even and let her soar!

British Aerospace/Aérospatiale Concorde

The Concorde is currently the world's only supersonic transport (SST). When it first flew in 1969, many supersonic airliners were on the drawing board. But, because of noise and environmental concerns, all the other projects were scrapped. Though only twenty Concordes were built, they have remained in service and continue to carry passengers around the world at supersonic speeds. Even at thirty years of age, the Concorde cruises two and a half times faster than other airliners, carrying passengers across the Atlantic Ocean in about three and a half hours.

The first studies for a supersonic transport date back to the mid-1950s, when the first jet-powered airliners were coming into service. Engineers could envision jet technology developing to a point that would enable passenger planes to cruise at supersonic speeds, and in the early 1960s, four countries began developing SSTs. In the United States, Boeing began work on an enormous, 300-passenger aircraft

The Concorde is operated by three people: the pilot, copilot, and a flight engineer who manages the aircraft's systems.

designed to fly at three times the speed of sound (Mach 3). Britain, France, and the Soviet Union, meanwhile, were developing smaller, 100- to 150-passenger versions designed to fly at Mach 2. Environmental concerns and economic considerations derailed the U.S. aircraft, and the British and French decided to pool their efforts in 1962. The joint effort, now named Concorde, took to the skies on March 2, 1969, but it had been beaten by the Soviet Tu-144, which, on December 31, 1968, had become the first SST to fly. Even after a major redesign, however, the Tu-144 was never introduced into continuous service because of technical issues and high operating costs. Whereas the Concorde, after six years of design development and certification testing, entered service in 1976.

Although both France and Britain had their own final assembly lines for Concorde, each country produced different parts. The British Aircraft Corporation (now British Aerospace) manufactured the nose, tail, and engine pods, while Aérospatiale in France made the center fuselage, wings, and landing gear. The engines were manufactured by Rolls-Royce, with assistance from the French engine company SNECMA. A unique moving nose section was developed that lowers to give the pilot an unobstructed view at low speed, and raises to decrease drag during supersonic flight. To compensate for the shift in aerodynamics that takes place between low and supersonic speed, additional tanks were placed in the nose and tail so that fuel could be shifted forward or aft for optimum balance. Similar to those in modern jet fighters, the engines incorporate supersonic inlets and nozzles, thrust reversers,

Supersonic flight takes about half the time of regular commercial airliners.

and afterburners. In addition, the Concorde cabin is more highly pressurized than that of any other passenger aircraft, as it cruises at an altitude almost twice that of conventional airliners.

Early in the development stage, SSTs had been seen as the next generation of airliner. But, as the planes got closer to production, concerns were expressed about the noise the powerful engines would produce during takeoff and landing, and the damage to the Earth's ozone layer the planes would inflict. To make matters worse, as the Concorde went into operation in the late 1970s, petroleum prices skyrocketed, rendering the fuel-hungry airliners even more expensive to run. As a result, the only airlines to purchase the airplanes were Air France and British Airways. (At one time, options for seventy aircraft were held by numerous airlines, but environmental and economic concerns resulted in most orders being canceled.) Today, although the only regularly scheduled service for these planes is between the cities of New York, London, Paris, and Washington, D.C., Concordes are frequently

SPECS

Length: 203 ft. 9 in.	
Height: 37 ft. 5 in.	
Wingspan: 83 ft. 10 in.	
Engines: Four Rolls Royce/ SNECMA Olympus 593 Mk 610 engines, 38,050 lb. thrust each	
Weight: 173,000 lb. empty, 408,000 lb. max.	
Max. Speed: Mach 2.04 (1,354 m.p.h.)	
Range: 4,090 mi.	
Max. Altitude: 60,000 ft.	

Why Not Faster?

Temperature is the main factor limiting aircraft speed. As an airplane goes faster, "skin friction" (the air rubs against the surface of the plane like your hands rubbing a carpet) increases the temperature of the hull. At the Concorde's 60,000-foot cruising altitude, the air temperature is –70°F. But air friction heats the outside surface of the plane to 250°F. Going any faster would require the Concorde to be built from something heavier and more expensive than aluminum.

chartered for specialty trips. They have maintained an impressive record of reliability and safety, with only one crash in over twenty years of operation.

Engineers around the world continue to develop the technologies to make SSTs quieter, more environmentally friendly, and more fuel-efficient. But although progress has been made, it is unlikely that another one will be produced until 2010 or later—something that makes the accomplishments of the Concorde team all the more impressive. The Concorde is, and will forever remain, a symbol of technology, speed, and the potential of air travel.

BRITISH AEROSPACE/AÉROSPATIALE CONCORDE

Rudder

Elevators

BRITISH AIRWAYS

FLYING TIPS: Before flying, make sure wings are flat and even, not warped. The plane flies best with a gentle toss angled downward. **If your plane dives:** Bend the elevators up a bit or throw the plane a little faster. **If your plane climbs, slows, then dives:** Bend the elevators down a bit or throw the plane a little slower. If that doesn't help, try slipping a paper clip over the nose. **If your plane veers:** Bend the rudder a little in the opposite direction of the unwanted turn (i.e., if your plane veers right, bend the rudder left, and vice versa).

Cut along heavy solid lines. Score, then fold in along dashed lines (so they're no longer visible); fold away along dotted lines. Glue like letter to like letter. For details, see page 62.

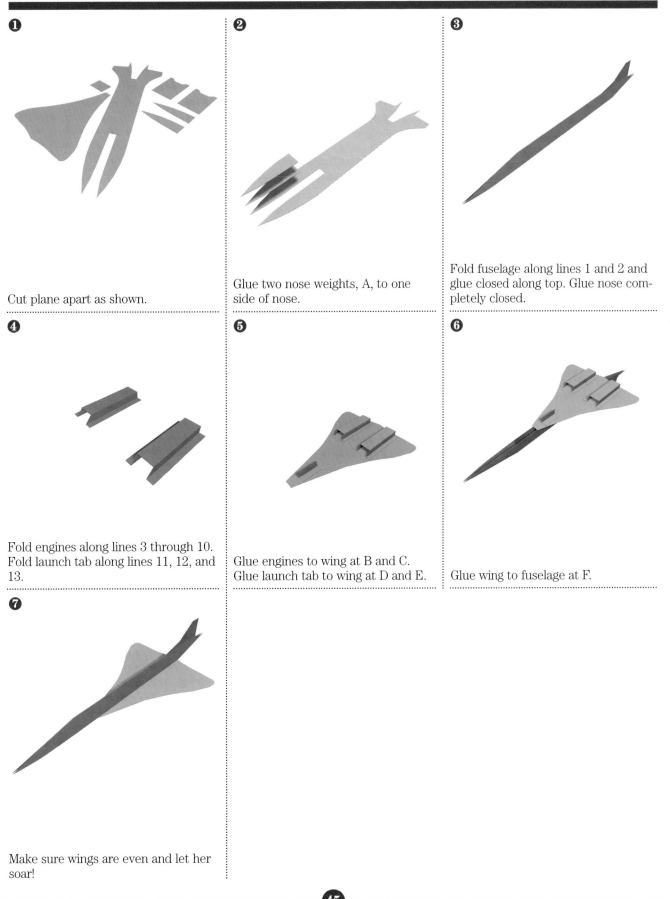

❶

Cut plane apart as shown.

❷

Glue two nose weights, A, to one side of nose.

❸

Fold fuselage along lines 1 and 2 and glue closed along top. Glue nose completely closed.

❹

Fold engines along lines 3 through 10. Fold launch tab along lines 11, 12, and 13.

❺

Glue engines to wing at B and C. Glue launch tab to wing at D and E.

❻

Glue wing to fuselage at F.

❼

Make sure wings are even and let her soar!

Boeing F-15 Eagle

All F-15 flight information is projected on a glass screen at eye level so the pilot doesn't have to look down at the cockpit instruments.

The F-15 has been the dominant fighter in the world since its introduction in 1976. Its genesis can be traced back to the Vietnam War, when America's primary fighter was the McDonnell Douglas F-4 Phantom. The F-4 had been designed to use air-to-air missiles exclusively, since it was believed that these new missiles would make dogfighting, and the need for maneuverability, a thing of the past. One of the lessons of the Vietnam conflict, however, was that missiles could not be used on every occasion. It was thus decided that future fight-

ers should again feature guns, and be designed for agility. At the same time, they would need to be big and fast to counter new planes being developed in the Soviet Union. The challenge would be to create a fighter that was large and fast, yet light and nimble.

McDonnell Douglas (now part of Boeing) won the contract for the new fighter in 1969, and used the latest technologies to meet the demanding requirements. Titanium and boron composites were used in the airframe for their strength and light weight. Extensive wind tunnel tests were performed to make the new

Air-to-Air Missiles

The F-15 can carry three different types of missiles for shooting down enemy fighters, all built by Raytheon. The AIM-7 Sparrow is a medium range (fifty miles) missile guided by the powerful radar of the F-15. The AIM-120 Advanced Medium Range Air-to-Air Missile (AMRAAM) is newer and has the ability to use its own onboard radar to locate and direct itself to the target. The AIM-9 Sidewinder is a short-range (ten miles) missile which homes in on the heat of the intended target. A new version of the Sidewinder called the AIM-9X is currently under development; it allows the pilot to fire at any enemy aircraft in his view, not just those at which the aircraft is pointed.

An F-15A Eagle launching an AIM-7 Sparrow missile

fighter fast and maneuverable. Lightweight engines were developed that were efficient enough to enable a long range, while producing enough thrust to accelerate the new plane vertically like a rocket. A powerful radar was developed to detect enemy fighters at a distance and to guide long-range missiles. The plane also incorporated a bubble canopy for increased visibility, simplified pilot controls, and a gun capable of shooting a hundred rounds per second, all designed to improve its dogfighting capability. The combined result of all these new technologies took flight for the first time in 1972 as the F-15 Eagle.

The F-15 matched expectations, with a top speed of two and a half times the speed of sound, a range of 2,400 miles, and the ability to carry eight air-to-air missiles or up to 23,000 pounds of bombs. The phenomenal performance of the aircraft has allowed it to set several climb-rate records, and has given the plane a combat record second to none. During Operation Desert Storm, F-15s shot down thirty-three of the thirty-five Iraqi airplanes downed. In fact, the F-15 has outperformed any other fighter, with a perfect combat record of 100 victories and zero defeats. Since its introduction, over 1,500 F-15s have been built for the Air Forces of the U.S., Japan, Israel, and Saudi Arabia.

The F-15 has continued to perform as the world's best fighter, thanks to ongoing improvements to both existing and newly manufactured Eagles. These include engines with more thrust, a more powerful radar, increased fuel capacity, the ability to carry new missiles and bombs, and even the ability for the autopilot to fly the plane just a few feet off the ground to avoid enemy detection. In fact, thanks to all these changes, the new planes being produced in St. Louis are quite different from the original models produced over twenty years ago. Although the Air Force is developing a new fighter, the F-22 Raptor, to replace the F-15, there is no doubt the Eagle will continue in service for decades to come.

SPECS

Length: 63.8 ft.
Height: 18.5 ft.
Wingspan: 42.8 ft.
Engines: Two P&W F100 turbofan engines in 29,000-lb. thrust class with afterburning
Weight: 45,000-lb. class, 81,000 lb. max. gross takeoff
Speed: Mach 2.5 class
Range: 2,400+ mi.
Altitude: 50,000+ ft.

Streak Eagle

Between January 16 and February 1, 1975, an F-15 Eagle dubbed the "Streak Eagle" set eight records for the minimum time needed to reach different altitudes. Each flight started with the plane stationary at the end of the runway, followed by a full-power climb to the target altitude. In one ascent, the Streak Eagle went from a stationary start to over seven miles high in less than one minute! And in several other flights, the plane accelerated through the sound barrier during a vertical climb.

The Streak Eagle was flown in its natural metal finish to reduce weight for the record-setting flights, but to protect it from corrosion the plane has since been painted in the gray color scheme of most operational F-15s.

BOEING F-15 EAGLE

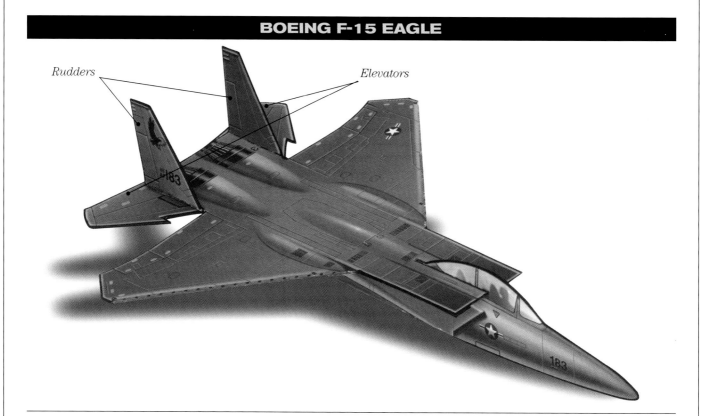

Rudders

Elevators

FLYING TIPS: Before flying, make sure wings are flat and even, not warped. Then bend the entire front edge of each wing gently downward. The plane flies best with a gentle toss angled downward. **If your plane dives:** Bend the elevators up a bit or throw the plane a little faster. **If your plane climbs, slows, then dives:** Bend the elevators down a bit or throw the plane a little slower. If that doesn't help, try slipping a paper clip over the nose. **If your plane veers:** Bend the rudder a little in the opposite direction of the unwanted turn (i.e., if your plane veers right, bend the rudder left, and vice versa).

Cut along heavy solid lines. Score, then fold in along dashed lines (so they're no longer visible); fold away along dotted lines. Glue like letter to like letter. For details, see page 62.

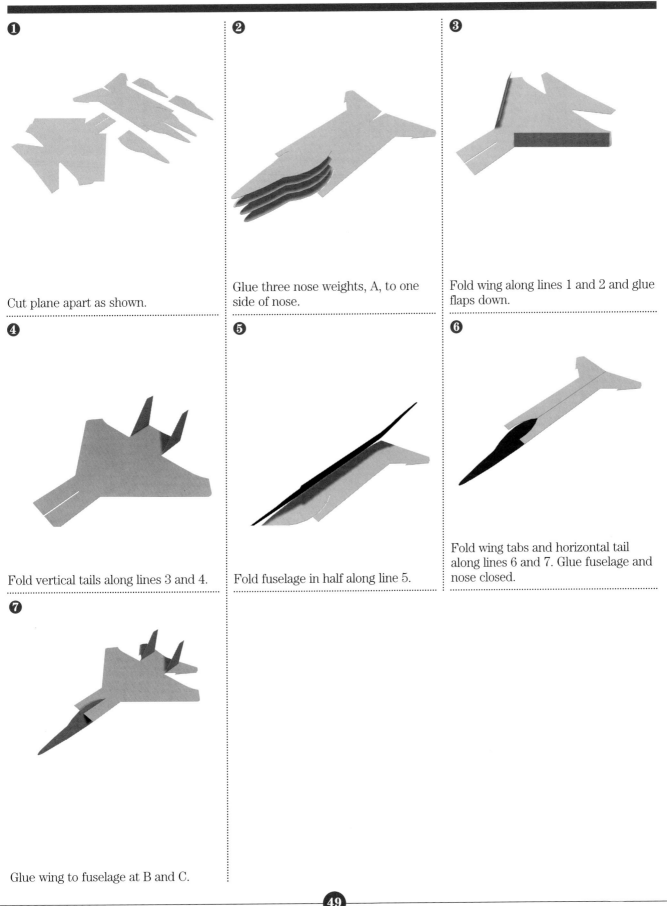

❶
Cut plane apart as shown.

❷
Glue three nose weights, A, to one side of nose.

❸
Fold wing along lines 1 and 2 and glue flaps down.

❹
Fold vertical tails along lines 3 and 4.

❺
Fold fuselage in half along line 5.

❻
Fold wing tabs and horizontal tail along lines 6 and 7. Glue fuselage and nose closed.

❼
Glue wing to fuselage at B and C.

Cessna 172 Skyhawk

The Cessna 172 Skyhawk is the most popular civilian aircraft ever built. Although it has never set any records for flying fast or far, its combination of speed, range, payload, and cost make it an outstanding airplane. In the year 2000—forty-four years after it was first flown—the 172 was produced in greater numbers than any other aircraft in the world.

The history of small aircraft dates back to the first airplane flown by the Wright brothers. Only a few years after the Wrights' 1903 flight, people around the world were trying to put flying machines into production. One of these was Clyde Cessna, whose first airplane, built in 1911, was a copy of a European model. Cessna continued making airplanes, incorporating as Cessna Aircraft Company in 1927. The popularity of light aircraft really boomed in the 1930s, when the Piper J-3 Cub dominated the market.

World War II caused major changes in the world of light aircraft. First, the large number of returning military personnel was viewed as an enormous market by manufacturers. Second, various aircraft companies had done very well as a result of wartime production. Cessna had been building aircraft in only small numbers before the war, but it became a larger and better company thanks to its wartime production contracts for thousands of training aircraft. After the war, Cessna

realized they needed to develop a new model, aimed at the new entry-level aviation market, that would pick up some of the slack left by the end of wartime production. Their solution was a basic two-seat airplane called the Cessna 120, soon followed by the deluxe 140.

Cessna was one of only a few aircraft companies to do well after the war, and continued to develop new models in order to sustain their competitive lead. In 1947, the company introduced the 170 (larger, with four seats), following up in 1952 with the 180 (bigger and more powerful). Up to this point, all Cessna aircraft had been "tail draggers" (i.e., had tail wheels), and many still had fabric-covered wings. By the 1950s, however, the company had fully switched to all-metal construction, as pilots demanded the low maintenance and solid feel of aluminum-covered aircraft. Next to come were the benefits of tricycle-style (nosewheel) landing gear, which made for safer landings and easier ground taxiing. In 1956, Cessna introduced tricycle versions of the 170 and the 180, designated the 172 and the 182. The 172 was an instant success, since it included all the features most pilots wanted—four seats, tricycle landing gear, good cruising speed—at a lower price than other aircraft with comparable features.

Cessna has continually improved the looks and performance of the 172 to keep it

SPECS—Cessna 172R

Length: 27 ft. 2 in.

Height: 8 ft. 11 in.

Wingspan: 36 ft. 1 in.

Engine:
One Textron Lycoming IO-360-L2A
160 BHP at 2,400 RPM

Weight: 1,639 lb. empty, 2,450 lb. max

Max. Speed: 141 m.p.h.

Range: 790 mi.

Max. Altitude: 13,500 ft.

up-to-date. In 1960, the company introduced the 172A, which switched from the original straight vertical tail to the more modern-looking, swept-back vertical tail. A deluxe version of the 172, the 172B, was introduced in 1961. This was the first 172 to be designated "Skyhawk," and all subsequent 172s have retained the name. And in 1962, the designers improved the Skyhawk's visibility by adding a rear window, creating the 172D. In addition to structural and ordered a version of the Skyhawk designated the T-41 Mescalero. Eventually the Army, as well as many foreign air forces, also selected the T-41 as a military trainer. By 1967, Cessna was convinced the 172 needed a major upgrade to remain competitive, and developed the 172J—essentially an entirely new plane with new wings and a more streamlined fuselage—as a replacement. At the last moment, however, it was decided that the old 172 would continue in pro

Cessna has built more airplanes than any other company in the world.

advances, Cessna began following the marketing practices of the automotive industry, introducing cosmetic changes, such as a new paint scheme, every year.

Cessna has also used the Skyhawk as the basis for several other successful models. A deluxe version of the 172 was introduced in 1958 as the Model 175 Skylark. In 1964, the United States Air Force recognized that the 172 would make a great primary trainer,

duction, and that the 172J would be introduced as the Cessna 177 Cardinal. In 1979, Cessna introduced yet another variation on the standard 172 known as the 172 Cutlass RG (Retractable [landing] Gear). Although many of the 172 derivatives have been very successful, the only one still in production is the basic 172.

During the 1980s, production slowed and the price of the 172 increased. In 1987, Cessna halted production on all piston-engine aircraft, including the Skyhawk. Cessna cited product liability for escalating prices of the aircraft beyond reasonable limits, but vowed to restore production if laws were enacted to limit such liability. After the requisite legal changes were enacted, the company kept its word and resumed production of the 172 in 1997.

Cessna currently produces two versions of the Skyhawk, the 172R and the more powerful 172S. Although very similar to the original, the new versions boast quieter engines, updated instruments, and an improved interior. Even in the year 2000, forty-four years after its introduction, the Skyhawk was being

Cars vs. Planes

The most popular light airplanes are built in the hundreds each year—364 Cessna 172s, for example, were produced in the year 2000. Automobiles are built in much greater numbers, with some models produced at a rate of over 100,000 per year.

built in greater numbers than any other aircraft. With over 37,000 having been manufactured to date, the 172 Skyhawk will forever be known as a truly great light aircraft—a tremendous combination of performance and value, and an enduring example of classic design.

CESSNA 172 SKYHAWK

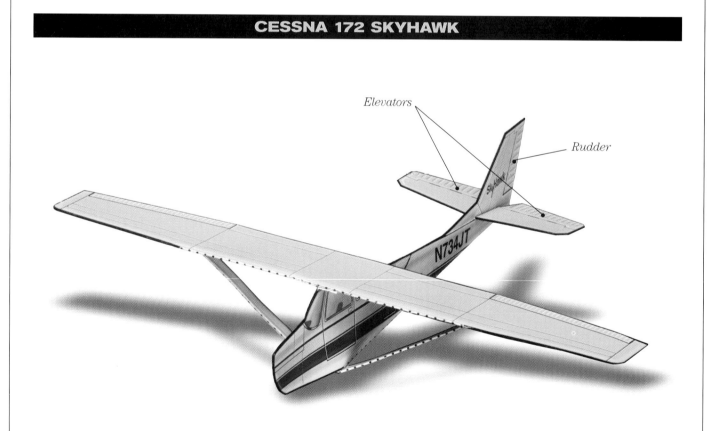

Elevators

Rudder

N734JT

FLYING TIPS: Before flying, make sure wings are flat and even, not warped. Then bend the entire front edge of each wing gently downward. The plane flies best with a gentle toss angled downward. **If your plane dives:** Bend the elevators up a bit or throw the plane a little faster. **If your plane climbs, slows, then dives:** Bend the elevators down a bit or throw the plane a little slower. **If your plane veers:** Bend the rudder a little in the opposite direction of the unwanted turn (i.e., if your plane veers right, bend the rudder left, and vice versa).

Cut along heavy solid lines. Score, then fold in along dashed lines (so they're no longer visible); fold away along dotted lines. Glue like letter to like letter. For details, see page 62.

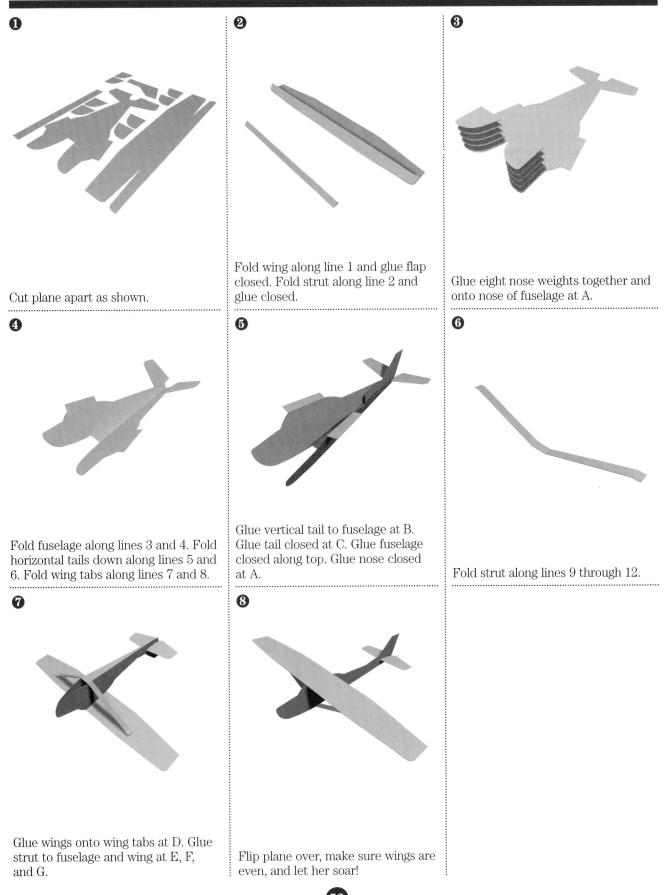

❶

Cut plane apart as shown.

❷

Fold wing along line 1 and glue flap closed. Fold strut along line 2 and glue closed.

❸

Glue eight nose weights together and onto nose of fuselage at A.

❹

Fold fuselage along lines 3 and 4. Fold horizontal tails down along lines 5 and 6. Fold wing tabs along lines 7 and 8.

❺

Glue vertical tail to fuselage at B. Glue tail closed at C. Glue fuselage closed along top. Glue nose closed at A.

❻

Fold strut along lines 9 through 12.

❼

Glue wings onto wing tabs at D. Glue strut to fuselage and wing at E, F, and G.

❽

Flip plane over, make sure wings are even, and let her soar!

Rutan/Yeager *Voyager*

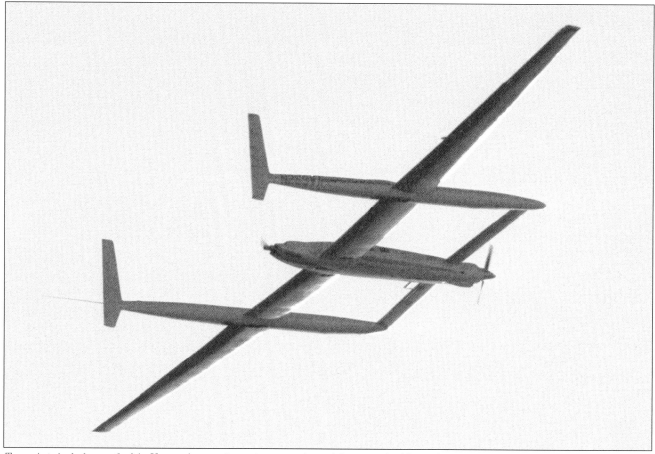

To maintain balance, fuel in Voyager's *seventeen storage tanks—eight on each side and one in the middle—had to be shifted from tank to tank during flight.*

Voyager is the only aircraft to have flown around the world without refueling. In fact, its nine-day, 25,000-mile journey in 1986 covered a distance twice that of the next-longest flight. *Voyager* was designed by Burt Rutan specifically to circle the globe, and was constructed mainly by him and the two pilots, Dick Rutan and Jeana Yeager. The aircraft had to be designed to extremes for such a long flight. It has a 110-foot wingspan, with a cabin so small that only one crew member can sit upright at a time. And it weighs less than a car, yet carries 7,000 pounds of fuel. *Voyager* made it around

the world, but just barely—it was down to less than eighteen gallons of fuel when it landed.

The *Voyager* saga started in February 1981, with Burt and Dick Rutan and Jeana Yeager sitting at a table discussing their dream projects. Dick and Jeana were experienced as pilots and with aircraft construction, while Burt, Dick's younger brother, was a famous aircraft designer looking to make his mark on history. Initially, Burt designed the plane as a giant wing with no tail, but further calculations showed this would not be big enough to hold the necessary 1,500 gallons of fuel. So the design evolved to include a large fuel tank on each side of the wing, which extended forward to hold the canard (see page 15) on the front, and the vertical tails in the back. Since the airplane would need over a week to complete the flight, both Dick and Jeana would take turns piloting while the other rested. The only way to make *Voyager* efficient enough was to build it entirely from the latest high-technology material—molded carbon graphite, which offered smooth, low-drag surfaces, light weight, and strength.

As Burt was designing the airplane, Dick and Jeana began the search for a sponsor to fund the construction and flight. When none came forward, they decided to do it on their own, working odd jobs and receiving small donations of material and help.

Construction began in early 1982. The expensive high-tech materials and the large size of the plane (the wings are as long as those on an airliner) required the team to invent new ways of building the parts, including making their own molds and ovens to cure them. Slowly, and helped by various individuals who volunteered their expertise and assistance, the enormous aircraft began to take shape in Hangar 77 at the Mojave Airport in the high desert of California. On June 22, 1984, the plane was finally ready and took to the air for the first time with Dick at the controls. Although one of the two engines had to be shut down in flight, and the controls felt a little strange, *Voyager* could fly. The next two and a half years were used to test and improve the craft—although it still became dangerously unstable with a full fuel load, it could be controlled with careful piloting.

On the morning of December 14, 1986, *Voyager* sat at the end of the runway at

Burt Rutan is known for designing aircraft of lightweight composite materials.

Edwards Air Force Base, filled with 1,000 pounds more fuel than it had ever carried before. Not only did the 10,000-pound craft have the longest takeoff distance in history, but the weight of the full fuel tanks made the wingtips drag on the pavement as it rolled down the runway, grinding them off. After a successful takeoff, the airplane, heavy with fuel and mildly unstable, headed southwest toward the equator. Day by day, *Voyager* made its way around the globe, with the pilots battling thunderstorms, troubleshooting mechanical problems like fuel-gauge errors and a broken autopilot, and fighting exhaustion. Finally, nine days, three minutes, and forty-five seconds after takeoff, *Voyager* returned to earth on the same runway from which it had started. The flight had consumed 98.5 percent of the fuel on board.

Voyager officially flew 24,986.7 miles and set eight world records. Today it deservedly resides at the entrance of the Smithsonian National Air and Space Museum in Washington, D.C. The fact that it was produced not by an expensive military program, but by a few remarkable individuals, makes it an even more amazing chapter in aviation history.

SPECS

Length:	*29 ft. 2 in.*
Height:	*10 ft. 3 in.*
Wingspan:	*110 ft. 8 in.*

Engines:
Front: Continental 0-240, 130 h.p.
Aft: Continental IOL-200, 110 h.p.

Weight:	*2,250 lb. empty, 10,000 lb. max.*
Speed:	*Average cruise, 116 m.p.h.*
Range:	*25,000 + mi.*
Altitude:	*20,500 ft. max. flown*

Yeager and Rutan on completing their voyage.

Roughing It

Every pound of weight on *Voyager* required a gallon of gasoline to fly around the world, so there were no luxuries on board, including no toilet. Instead, waste was collected in plastic bags. Since tossing them overboard risked damage to the rear propeller, all bags were stored in a compartment for the duration of the flight. Rutan and Yeager's meals were eaten cold as there was no way to heat anything up.

The space was so cramped that you couldn't stand up. One person sat in the pilot's seat and the other lay beside it.

RUTAN/YEAGER *VOYAGER*

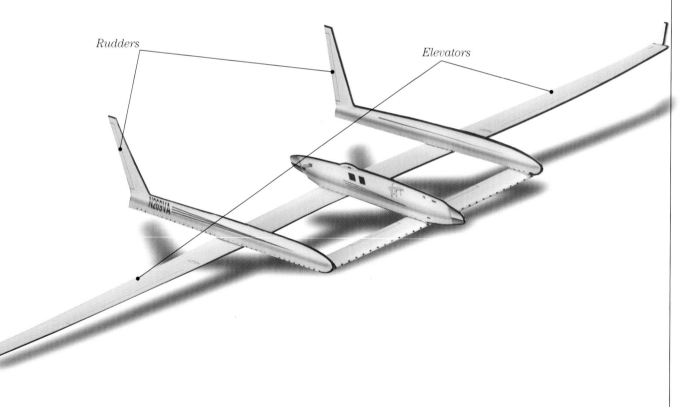

Rudders

Elevators

FLYING TIPS: Before flying, make sure wings are flat and even, not warped. Then bend the entire front edge of each wing gently downward. The plane flies best with a gentle toss angled downward. **If your plane dives:** Bend the elevators up a bit or throw the plane a little faster. **If your plane climbs, slows, then dives:** Bend the elevators down a bit or throw the plane a little slower. **If your plane veers:** Bend the rudder a little in the opposite direction of the unwanted turn (i.e., if your plane veers right, bend the rudder left, and vice versa).

Cut along heavy solid lines. Score, then fold in along dashed lines (so they're no longer visible); fold away along dotted lines. Glue like letter to like letter. For details, see page 62.

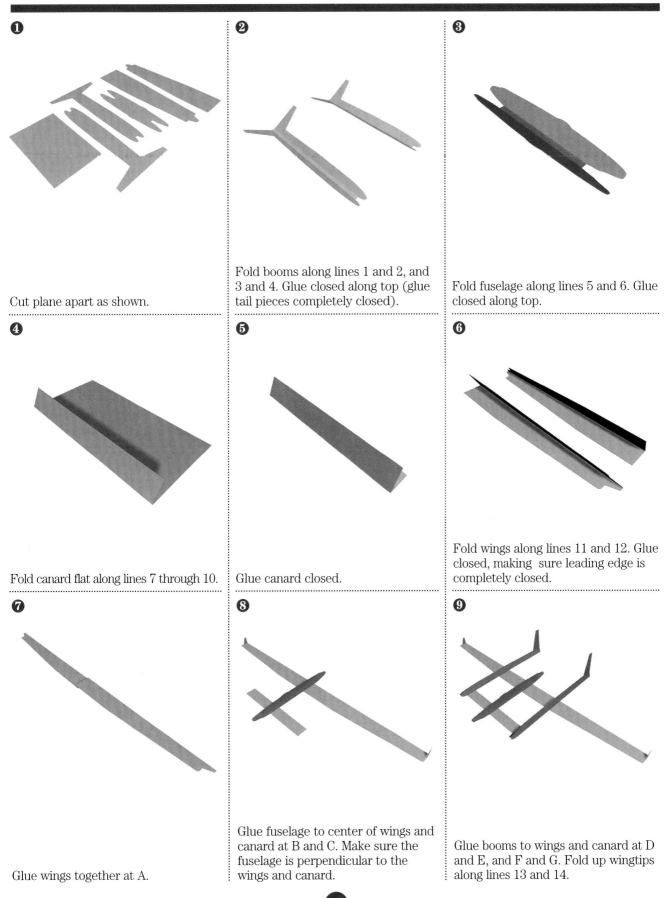

❶

Cut plane apart as shown.

❷

Fold booms along lines 1 and 2, and 3 and 4. Glue closed along top (glue tail pieces completely closed).

❸

Fold fuselage along lines 5 and 6. Glue closed along top.

❹

Fold canard flat along lines 7 through 10.

❺

Glue canard closed.

❻

Fold wings along lines 11 and 12. Glue closed, making sure leading edge is completely closed.

❼

Glue wings together at A.

❽

Glue fuselage to center of wings and canard at B and C. Make sure the fuselage is perpendicular to the wings and canard.

❾

Glue booms to wings and canard at D and E, and F and G. Fold up wingtips along lines 13 and 14.

Rockwell International Shuttle Spacecraft

Special ceramic tiles protect the orbiter from the heat generated during reentry into the Earth's atmosphere.

In the late '60s and early '70s, during the Apollo lunar space missions, the National Aeronautics and Space Administration (NASA) started planning the next generation of space travel. NASA wanted a new type of spacecraft capable of making cost-effective trips into orbit, carrying people and cargo on a regular basis. Studies indicated the best way to achieve this was to design a reusable spacecraft that could launch into space like a rocket but glide back to Earth and land like a plane. Various companies designed prototypes, and in 1972 NASA selected Rockwell International to design their new Space Transportation System (STS), which would later be called the space shuttle.

The vehicle they designed is very similar to the shuttles currently in use. As the shuttles do today, it included an orbiter, an external fuel tank, and two solid rocket boosters. Only the orbiter, which contained a crew compartment for up to eight astronauts, and a sixty-foot-long cargo bay, was designed to go into space. The solid rocket boosters were designed to parachute into the ocean two minutes after launch, to be recovered and reused. The only part of the vehicle that could not be reused was the large external fuel tank. About eight minutes into flight and just short of reaching Earth orbit—the point at which the shuttle, traveling 17,000 miles an hour, can coast around the Earth—the depleted external tank was designed to separate from the orbiter, falling and burning up in the atmosphere.

The first orbiter, named *Enterprise,* was a test vehicle which had its maiden voyage on August 12, 1976, at Edwards Air Force Base in California. The orbiter was mounted on top of a specially modified Boeing 747, which climbed to over 20,000 feet and released the shuttle for a five-minute test flight to demonstrate the orbiter's ability to glide and land like an airplane. The same 747 is now used to transport the orbiter across the country when needed. The *Enterprise* would make four more flights to check out all systems and performance characteristics before being used for ground tests, such as vibration studies and launch-complex fit checks. The *Enterprise* was retired, and donated in November 1985 to the Smithsonian National Air and Space Museum.

The first flight into space was by the shuttle *Columbia,* launching from Kennedy Space Center in Florida on April 12, 1981. It orbited the Earth thirty-six times while conducting system checks before landing at Edwards Air Force Base on April 14. In the following two years, *Columbia* completed four additional flights into space before being joined by the next orbiter, *Challenger.* By the end of 1985, the orbiters *Discovery* and *Atlantis* had also become operational.

On January 28, 1986, the *Challenger* began the shuttle program's twenty-fifth mission, carrying seven astronauts. Tragically, it exploded seventy-three seconds after launch. Unusually low temperatures the evening before the launch caused a solid rocket booster seam to open, allowing a hot jet of gas to burn through the external fuel tank. The shuttle fleet was grounded for two years, during which NASA made extensive modifications to the spacecraft as well as procedure changes prior to launch. Shuttle flight resumed in September 1988 when *Discovery* set out on a four-day mission. *Endeavour* was the last orbiter constructed, built to replace *Challenger,* and it had its first voyage in February 1992.

The space shuttle has transported a wide variety of payloads into orbit. It has launched many commercial, military, and scientific satellites, including the Hubble Space Telescope. On some missions, crew members conducted life-science experiments that included studies of plants' and animals' reaction to zero gravity. These were done in a removable module called Spacelab, a large pressurized laboratory that can be placed

Shuttle Facts— the First Twenty Years

- 100 launches
- 2½ years in space
- 624 crew members
- 3 million lbs. of payload to orbit
- 2 dozen payloads returned to Earth
- 60 satellites deployed
- Shuttle launches:

Orbiter	Launches
Columbia	26
Challenger	10
Discovery	28
Atlantis	22
Endeavour	14

SPECS

Length: 122 ft. 1 in.	
Height: 56 ft. 7 in.	
Wingspan: 78 ft. 1 in.	
Engines: Three Rocketdyne SSME 394,000-lb. thrust each	
Empty Weight: 171,000 lb.	
Max. Speed: 17,600 m.p.h.	
Range: 7,000,000 mi. (280 orbits)	
Max. Altitude: 400 mi.	

in the cargo bay. Other missions' aims were to repair or retrieve disabled satellites. In December 1998, the shuttle began delivering components of the International Space Station (ISS). The shuttle will be the primary spacecraft used to deliver and assemble the ISS, with a total of thirty-seven missions planned to complete the project.

In October 2000, *Discovery* completed the one hundredth space shuttle mission. Since the shuttle's inception, NASA has continually updated and modified the spacecraft to keep up with new technology for better safety and reliability. These advances include improvements to the landing gear, computer systems, crew escape systems, and engines. Looking into the future, NASA is currently conducting studies to define a replacement for the shuttle and expand manned space travel. Nonetheless, the shuttle will continue to be the United States' only manned space vehicle until at least the year 2010. It has established itself as one of the greatest manned space vehicles in history.

ROCKWELL INTERNATIONAL SHUTTLE SPACECRAFT

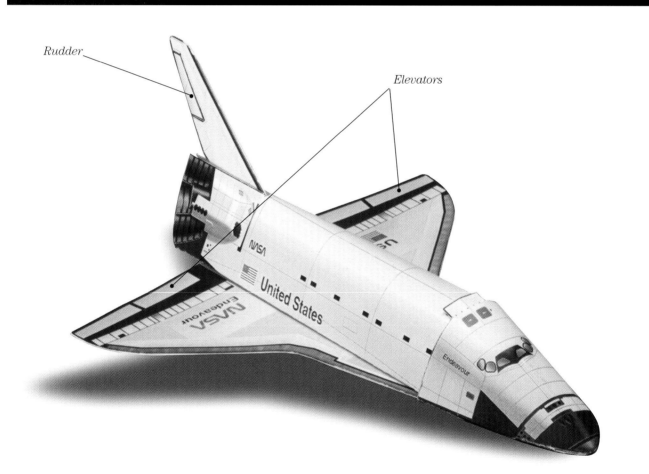

Rudder

Elevators

FLYING TIPS: Before flying, make sure wings are flat and even, not warped. The plane flies best with a gentle toss angled downward. **If your plane dives:** Bend the elevators up a bit or throw the plane a little faster. **If your plane climbs, slows, then dives:** Bend the elevators down a bit or throw the plane a little slower. **If your plane veers:** Bend the rudder a little in the opposite direction of the unwanted turn (i.e., if your plane veers right, bend the rudder left, and vice versa).

Cut along heavy solid lines. Score, then fold in along dashed lines (so they're no longer visible); fold away along dotted lines. Glue like letter to like letter. For details, see page 62.

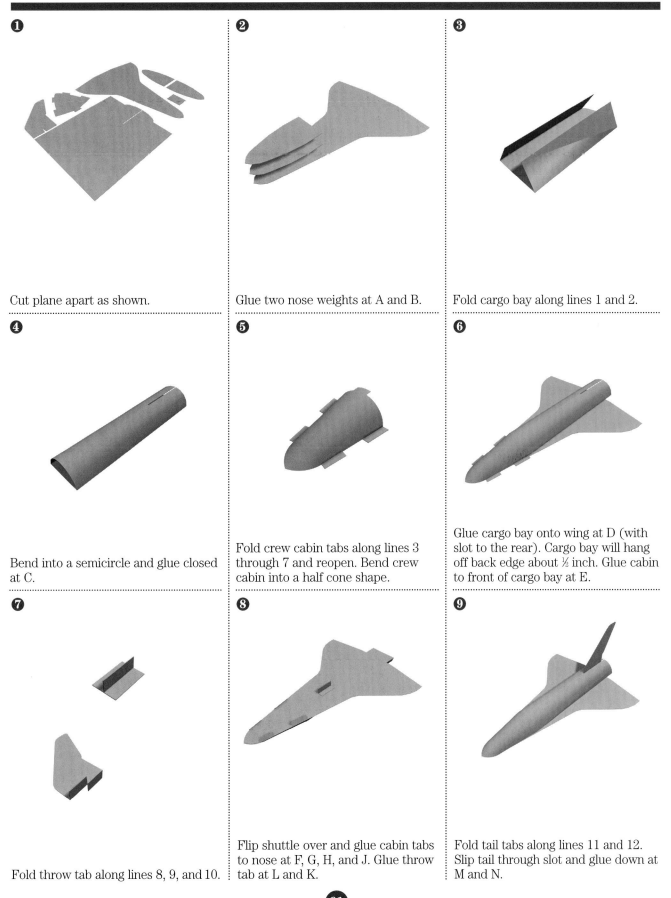

❶ Cut plane apart as shown.

❷ Glue two nose weights at A and B.

❸ Fold cargo bay along lines 1 and 2.

❹ Bend into a semicircle and glue closed at C.

❺ Fold crew cabin tabs along lines 3 through 7 and reopen. Bend crew cabin into a half cone shape.

❻ Glue cargo bay onto wing at D (with slot to the rear). Cargo bay will hang off back edge about ½ inch. Glue cabin to front of cargo bay at E.

❼ Fold throw tab along lines 8, 9, and 10.

❽ Flip shuttle over and glue cabin tabs to nose at F, G, H, and J. Glue throw tab at L and K.

❾ Fold tail tabs along lines 11 and 12. Slip tail through slot and glue down at M and N.

Making and Flying the Planes

CONSTRUCTION HINTS

The airplane patterns in this book are all marked with dashed, dotted, and solid lines that will guide you while you're constructing the planes. The dark solid lines are cut lines, and the first step in making each plane is to cut out all the parts.

The dashed and dotted lines are fold lines, but there is an essential difference between them. The dashed lines are what we call "fold-in" lines. This means that these lines will be on the inside of a crease, and you will not be able to see them once the plane is folded up. The dotted lines are "fold-away" lines—they will be visible after the fold is completed. Often, the dotted lines are simply guides on the reverse side of the dashed lines to help ensure that you're folding in the right place. Fold in on the dashed lines in the order that they're numbered. It's easiest to make a fold by first using a ruler and a ballpoint pen to draw (score) the lines.

Elevator Adjustment

Up Elevator

Down Elevator

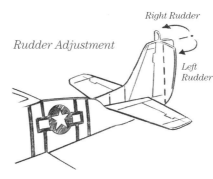

Rudder Adjustment

Right Rudder

Left Rudder

Letters indicate where separate parts are glued together (for example, you'll glue part A to part A, B to B, and so on). It's best to use rubber cement or white glue and to press the parts together on a hard surface like a table to ensure the glued pieces come out flat. Sometimes it's useful to use small binder clips to hold parts of the plane together while the glue dries.

FINE-TUNING HINTS

Like the originals, these planes are all excellent flyers. The following tips will help you get the best flight performance.

All paper airplanes need some adjustment. The most important thing to do is to hold the plane facing you and make sure that everything looks straight and the wings are even. If you find any parts that are warped or wavy, carefully bend the parts until they are straight.

In addition, most planes will require adjustments to the elevator and rudder for smooth flights. If the aircraft nosedives, bend the elevator up a little. If the plane stalls (climbs and then suddenly drops), bend the elevator down a little. For most of the planes in this book, the elevator is located on the back of the horizontal tail, as it is on real airplanes. If your plane is veering off in one direction or the other, use the rudder to make it fly straight. Bend the rudder to the right to correct a left turn (when viewed from behind), and to the left to correct a right turn. The rudder is usually located at the back of the vertical tail. If you still have difficulty making an airplane fly smoothly, try adding a small paper clip to the nose of the aircraft.

Making the Stands

Each plane comes with a stand to display it. Once you construct the stands you will need to attach the planes either permanently with glue, or temporarily with either a rolled piece of tape, double-stick tape, or a small piece of reusable adhesive putty. Each plane shows where it should attach to the stand. All of the planes except for the F-15 and the Bell X-1 rest on top of the stands. The fuselages of the F-15 and the Bell X-1 rest between the top tabs on the stands. Slip a piece of adhesive on each side of the tabs, and slip the fuselage in where indicated.

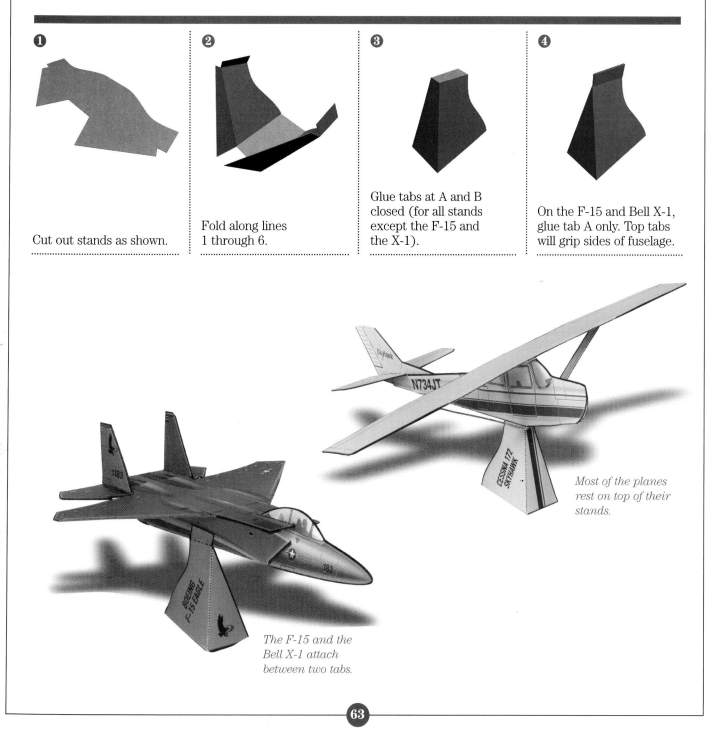

❶ Cut out stands as shown.

❷ Fold along lines 1 through 6.

❸ Glue tabs at A and B closed (for all stands except the F-15 and the X-1).

❹ On the F-15 and Bell X-1, glue tab A only. Top tabs will grip sides of fuselage.

Most of the planes rest on top of their stands.

The F-15 and the Bell X-1 attach between two tabs.

The Hangar

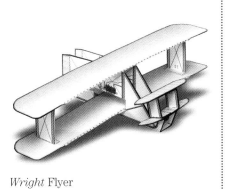

Wright Flyer

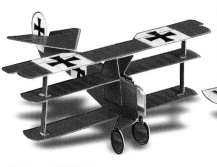

Fokker Dr.I Triplane

Ryan NYP–Spirit of St. Louis

Douglas DC-3

P-51 Mustang

Bell X-1

Boeing 747

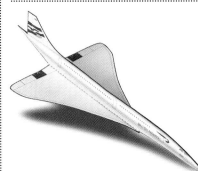

Concorde

Boeing F-15 Eagle

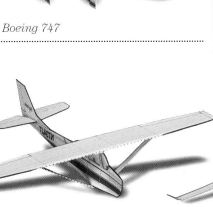

Cessna 172 Skyhawk

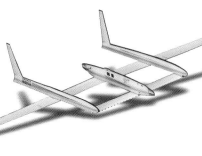

Rutan/Yeager Voyager

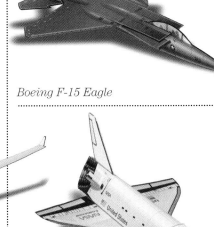

Space Shuttle

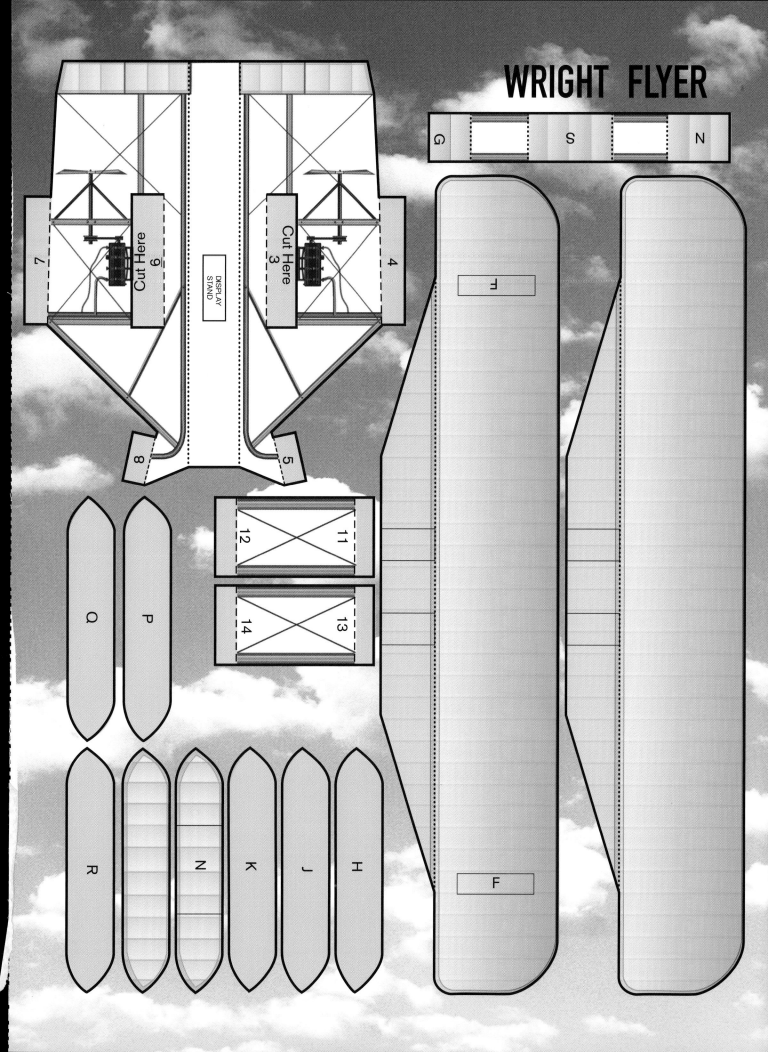

WRIGHT FLYER

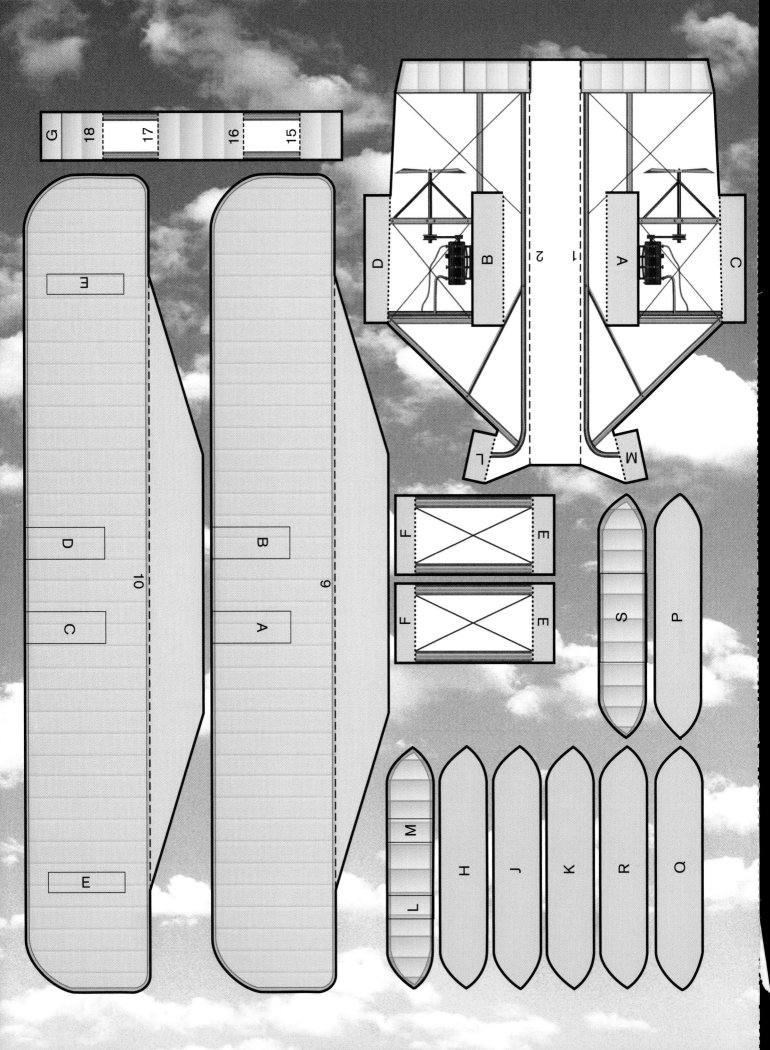

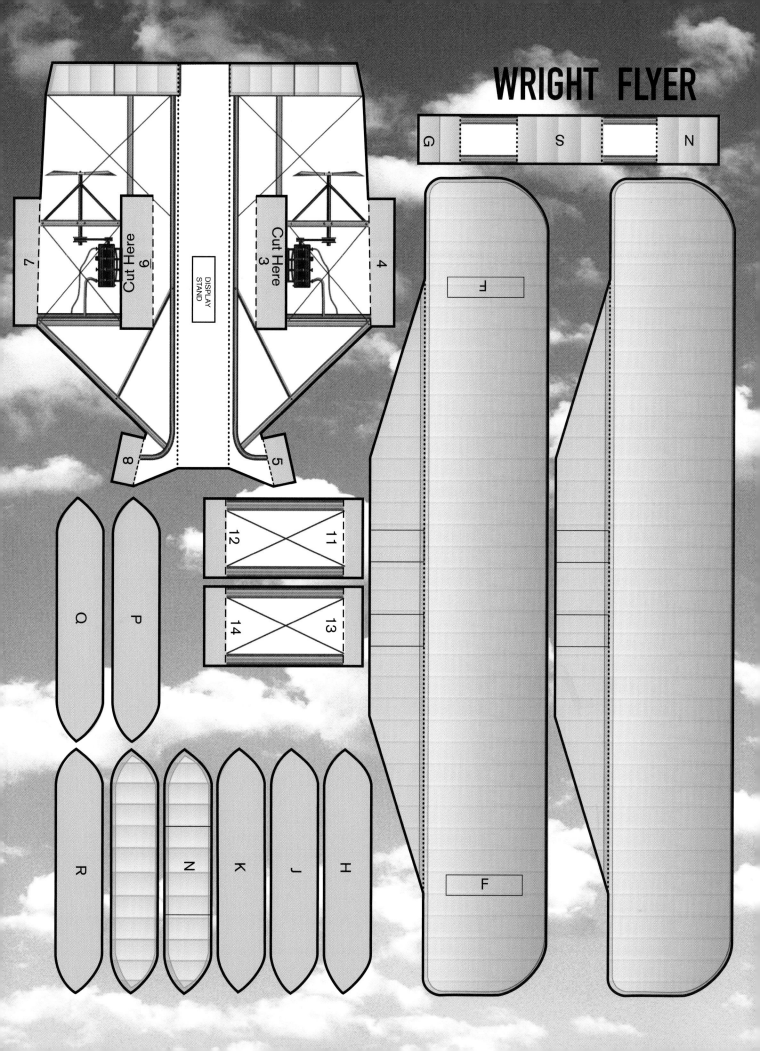

WRIGHT FLYER

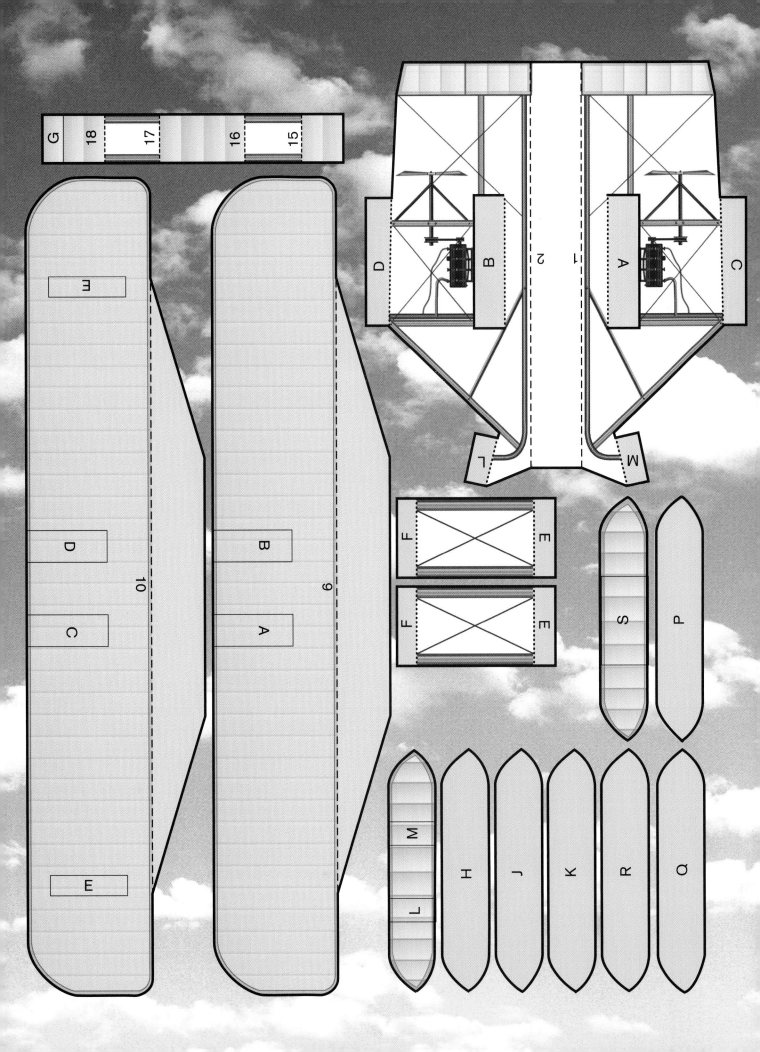

FOKKER DR.I

FOKKER DR.I

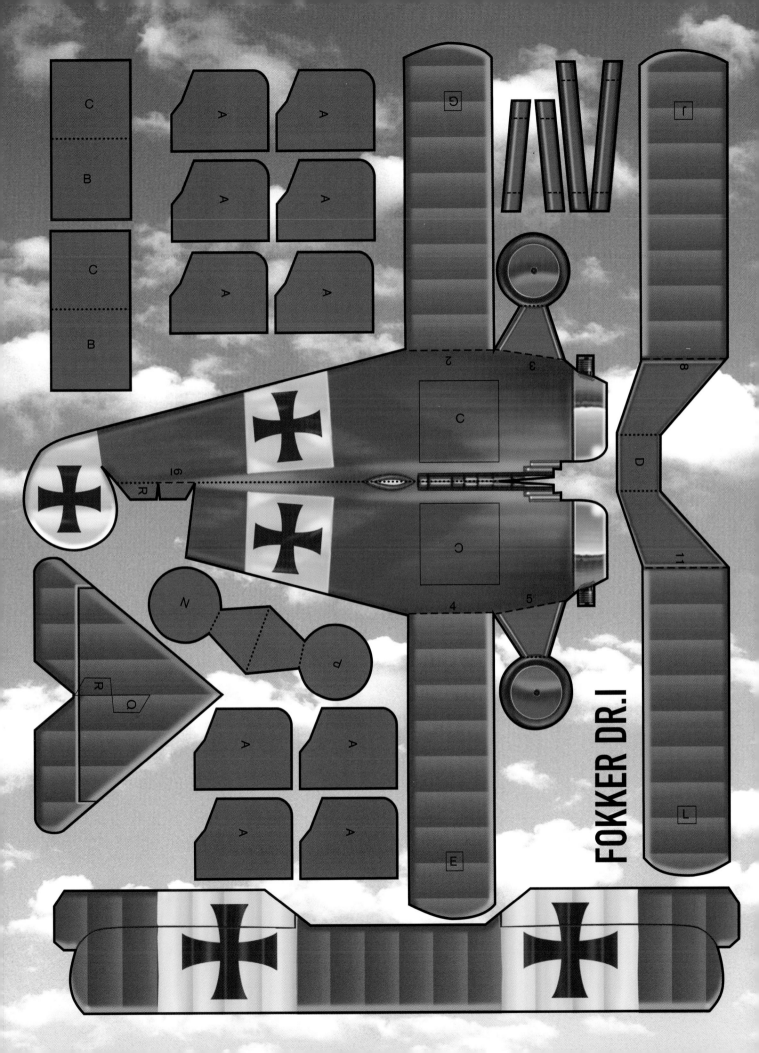

FOKKER DR.I

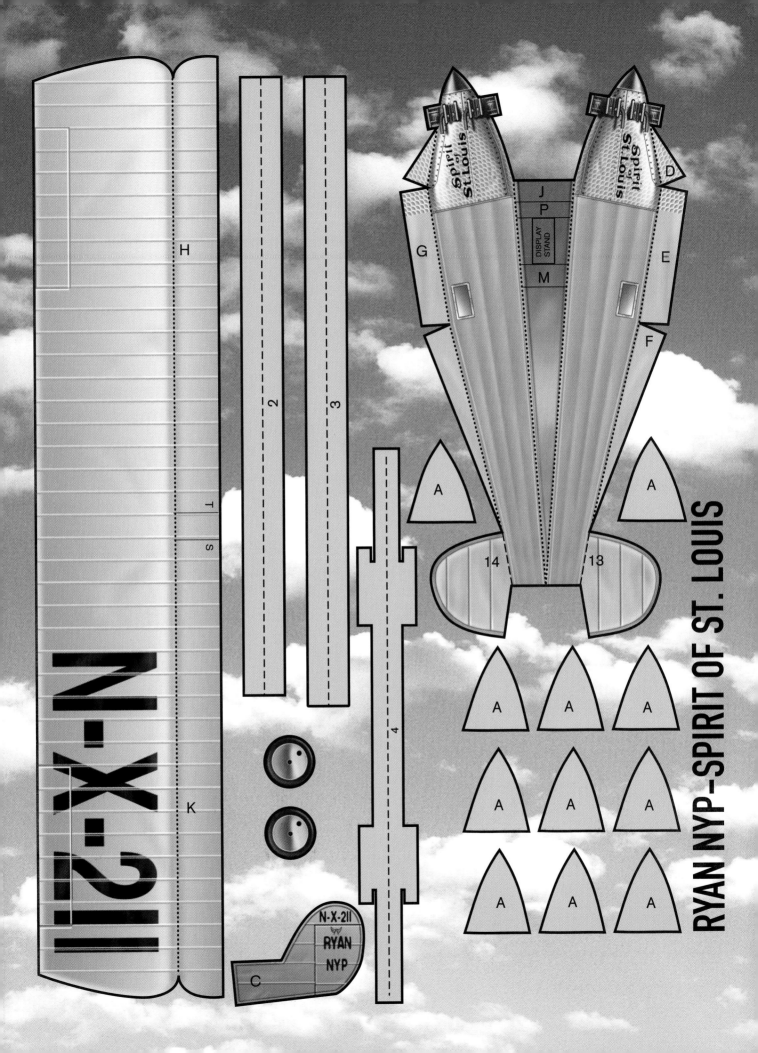

N-X-211

RYAN NYP–SPIRIT OF ST. LOUIS

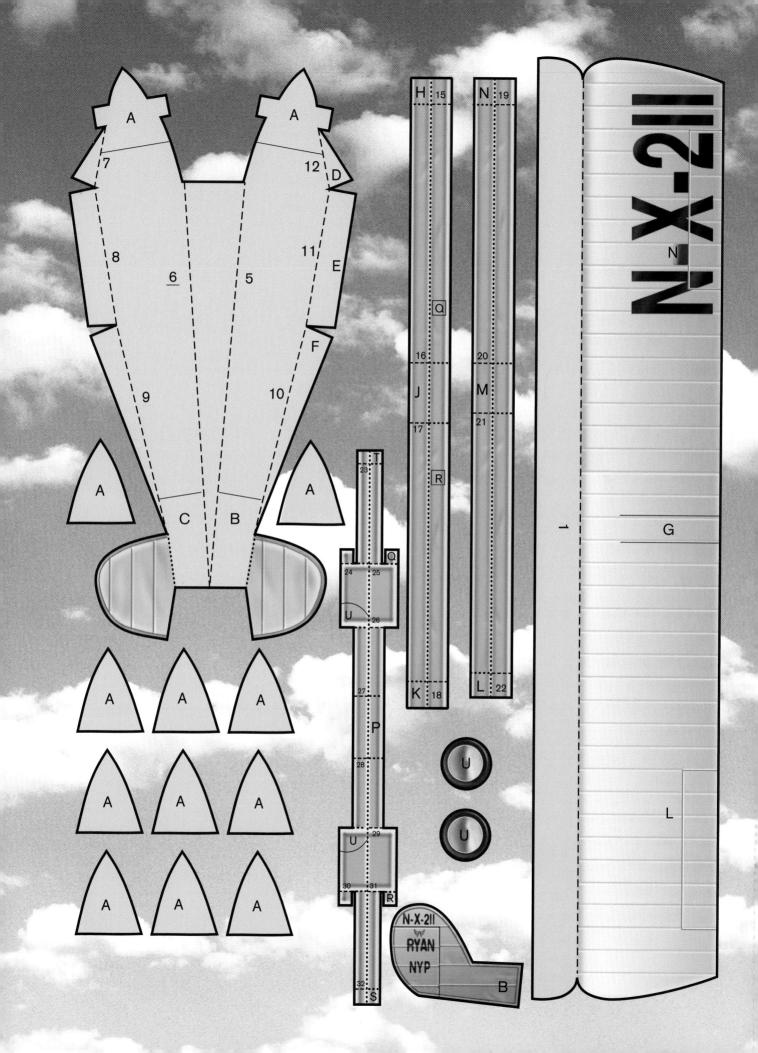

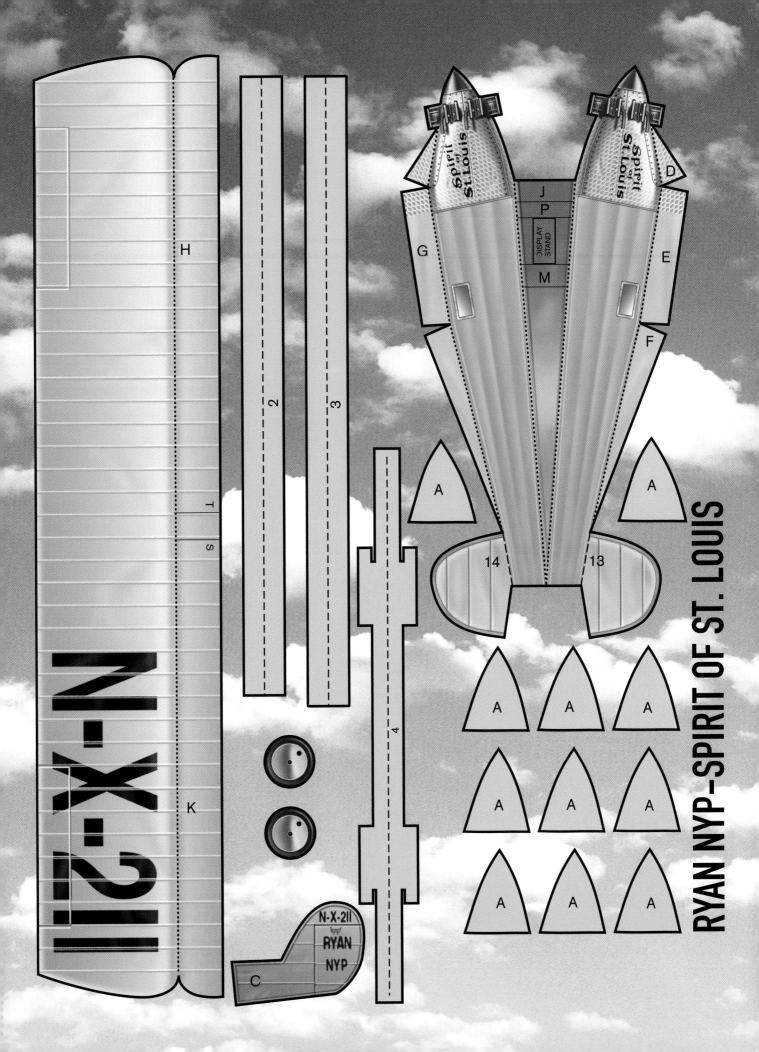

N-X-211

RYAN NYP–SPIRIT OF ST. LOUIS

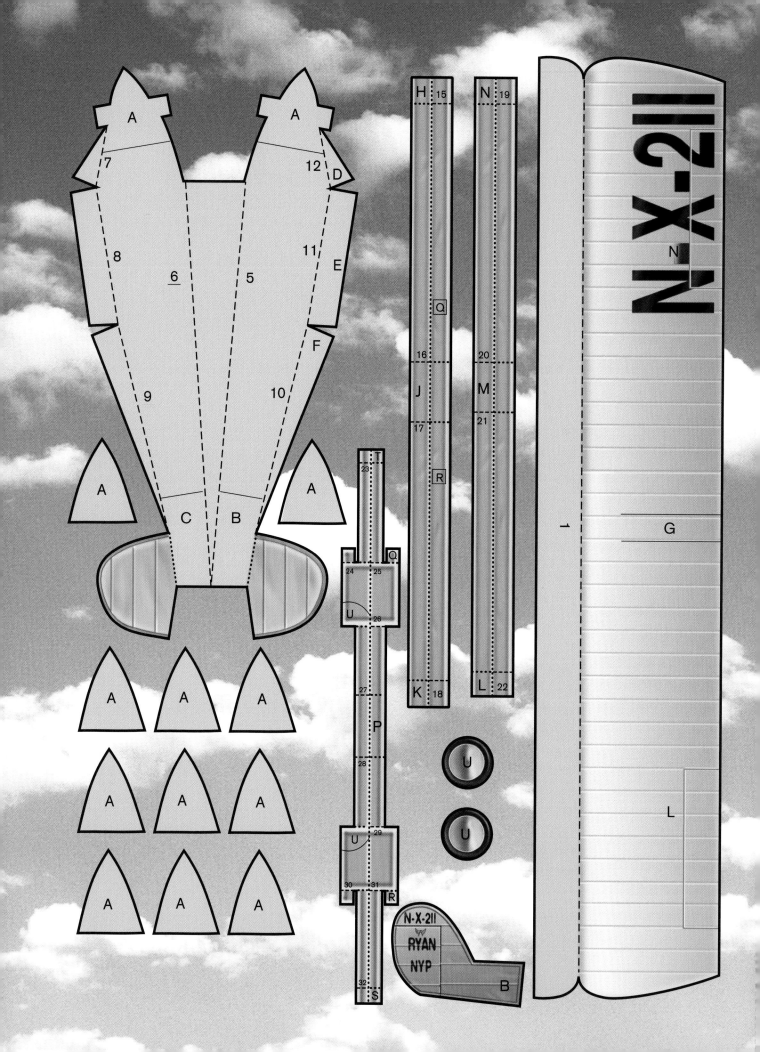

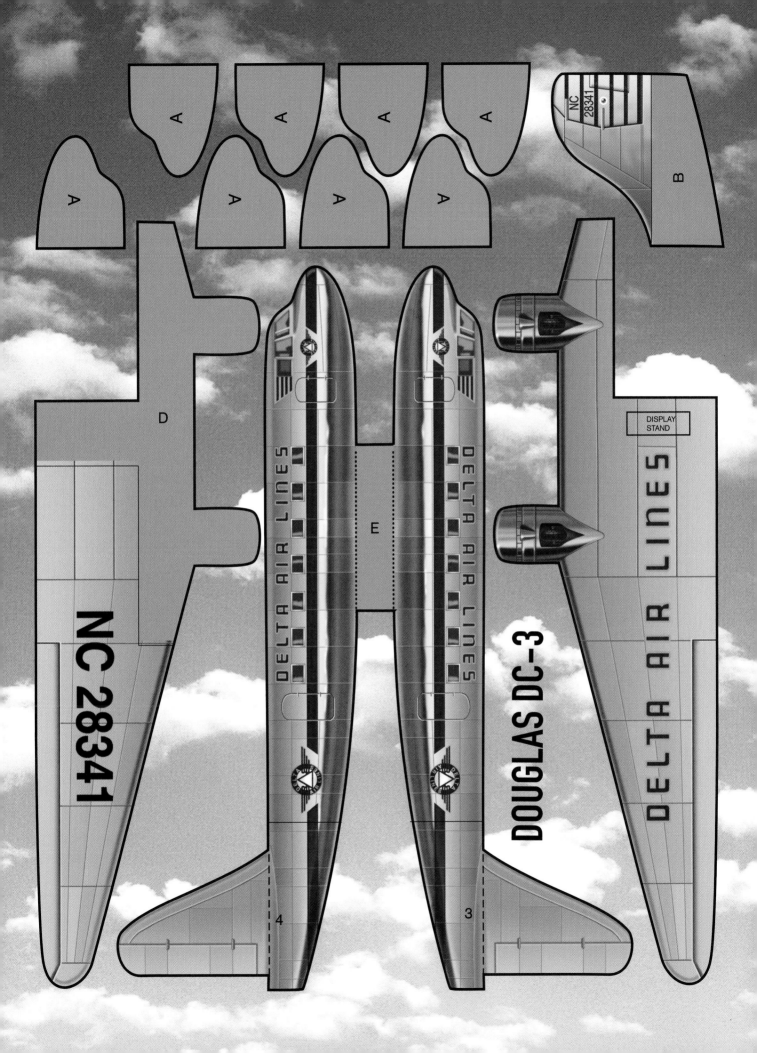

A

A

A

A

A

A

A

A

B

NC
28341

D

DISPLAY
STAND

E

NC 28341

DOUGLAS DC-3

DELTA AIR LINES

DELTA AIR LINES

DELTA AIR LINES

DELTA AIR LINES

4

3

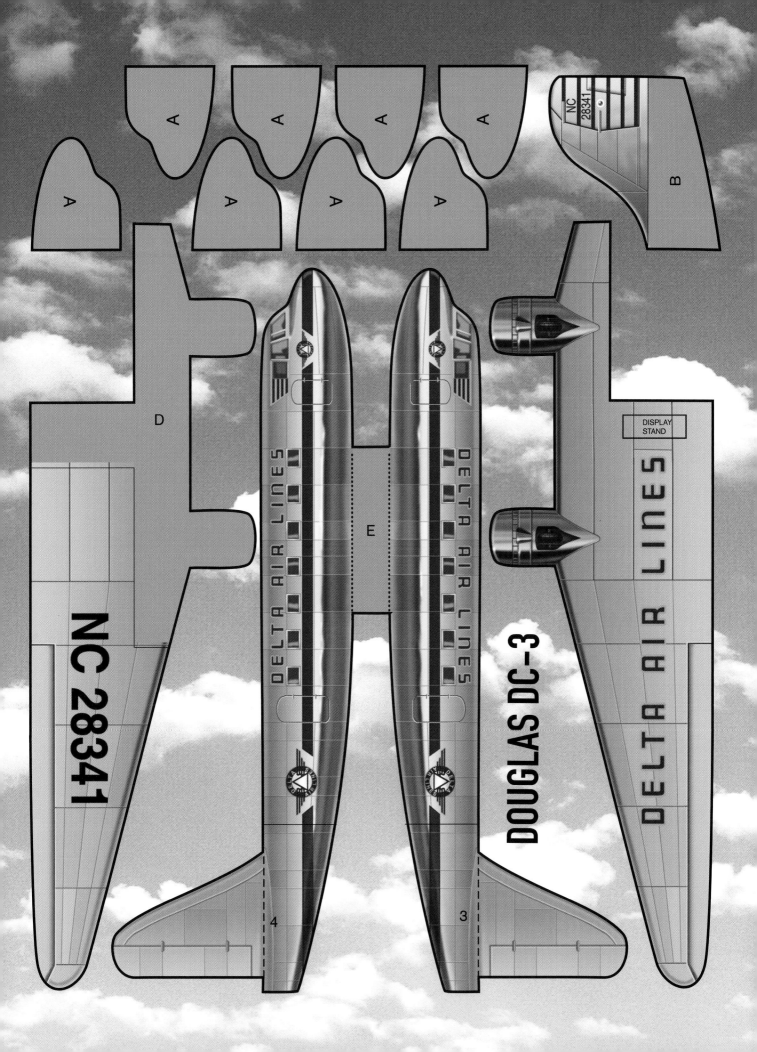

NC 28341

DELTA AIR LINES

DOUGLAS DC-3

DELTA AIR LINES

DISPLAY STAND

A A A A A

A A A A

B

D

E

4 3

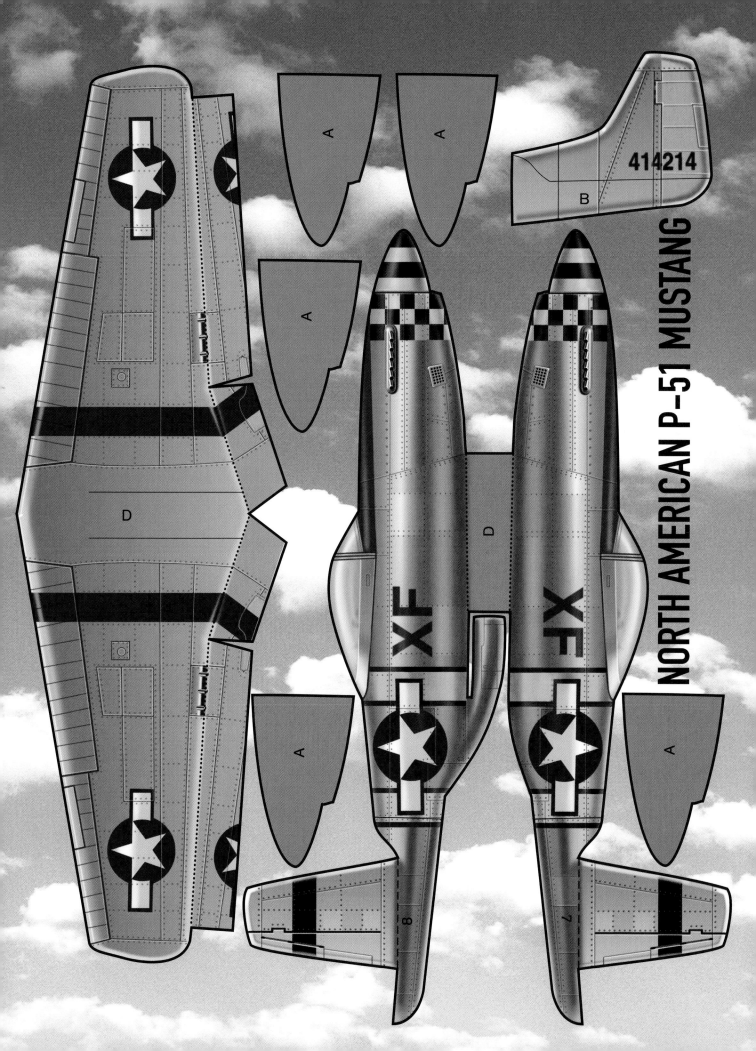

NORTH AMERICAN P-51 MUSTANG

414214

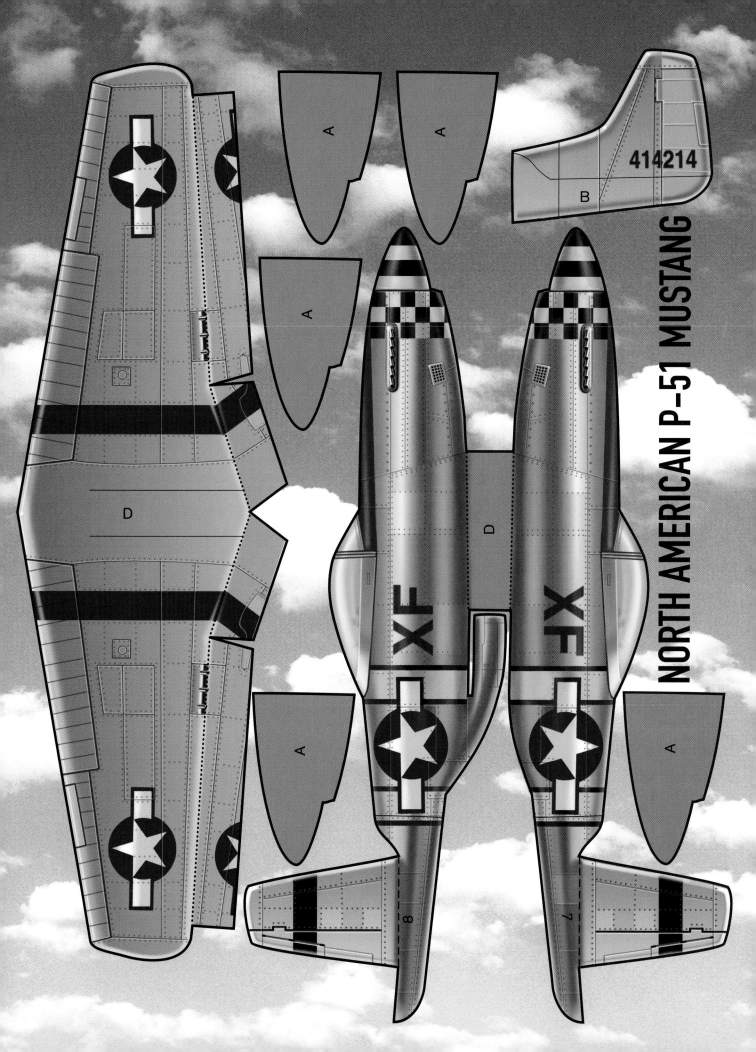

NORTH AMERICAN P-51 MUSTANG

414214

XF
XF

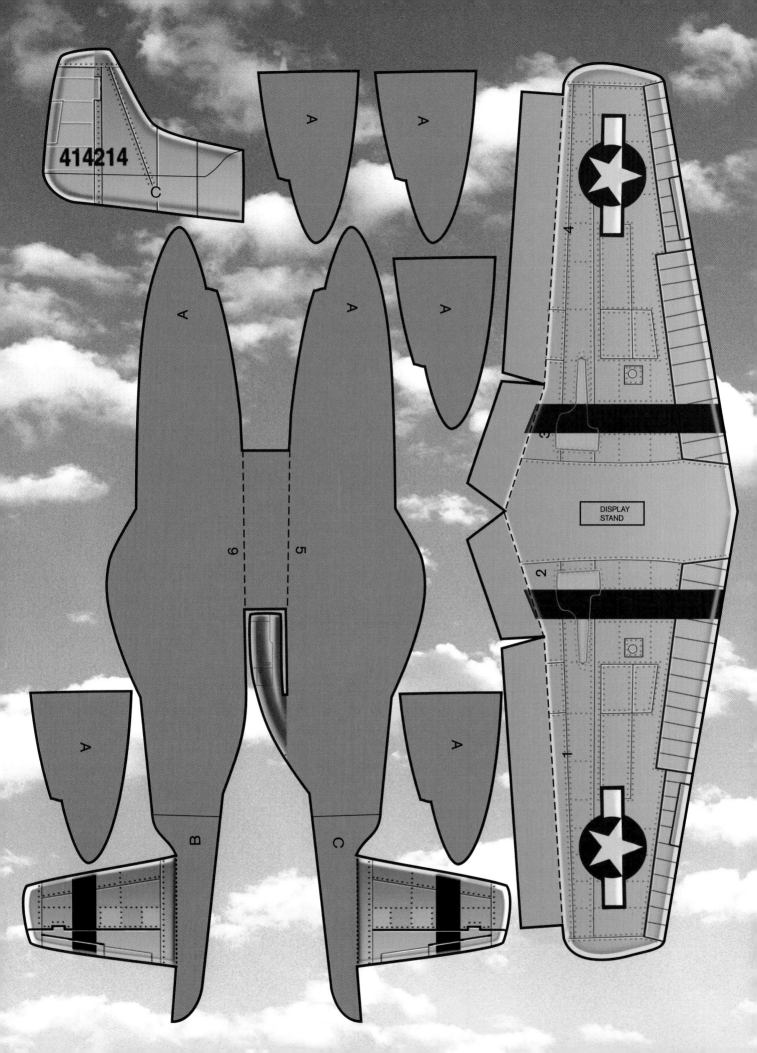

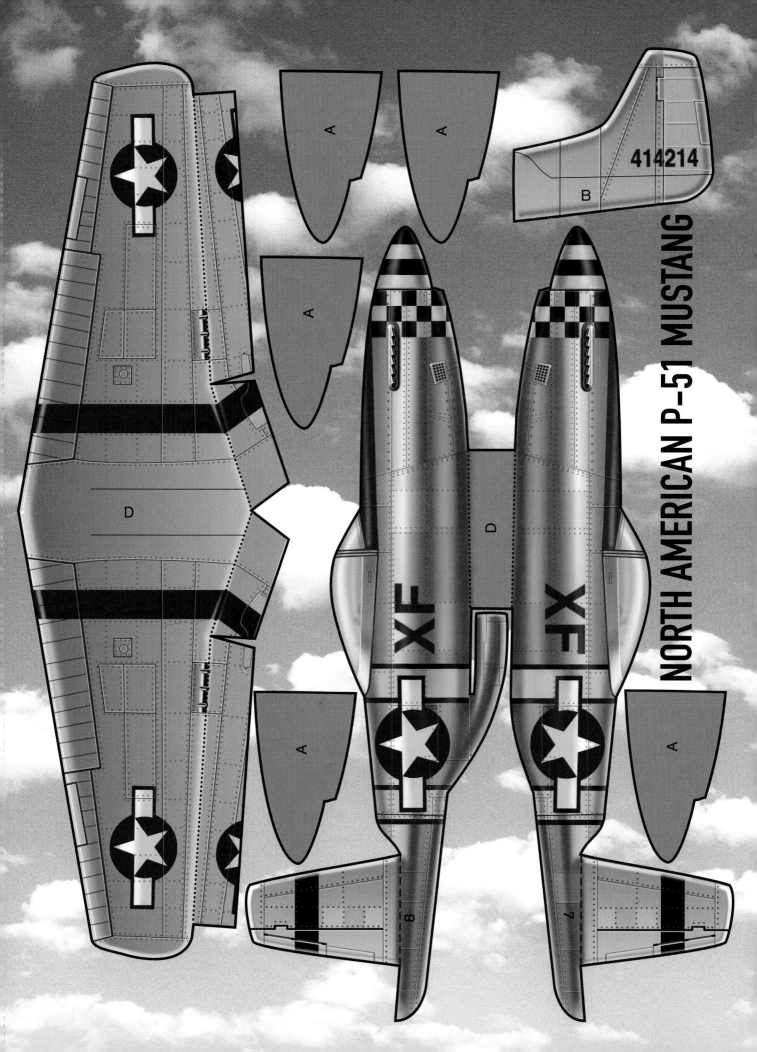

NORTH AMERICAN P-51 MUSTANG

414214

A A A A A B D D XF XF 8 7

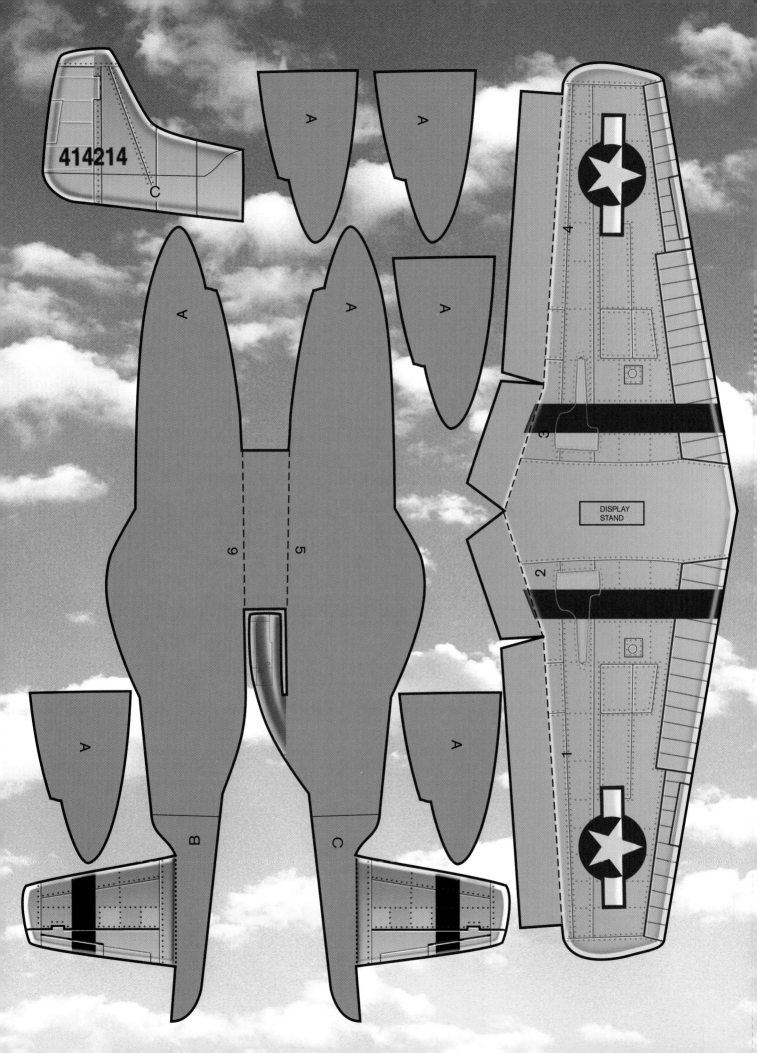

414214

DISPLAY
STAND

BELL X-1

BELL X-1

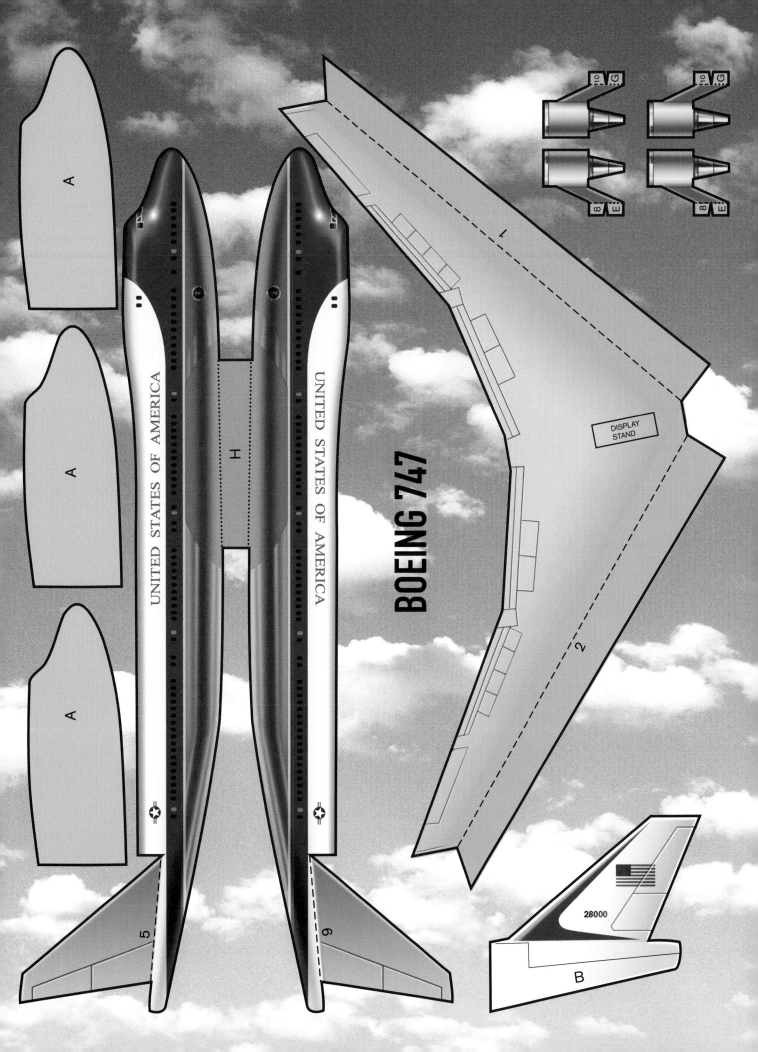

BOEING 747

A

A

A

UNITED STATES OF AMERICA

UNITED STATES OF AMERICA

H

DISPLAY
STAND

5

6

B

28000

G 10

E 8

G 10

E 8

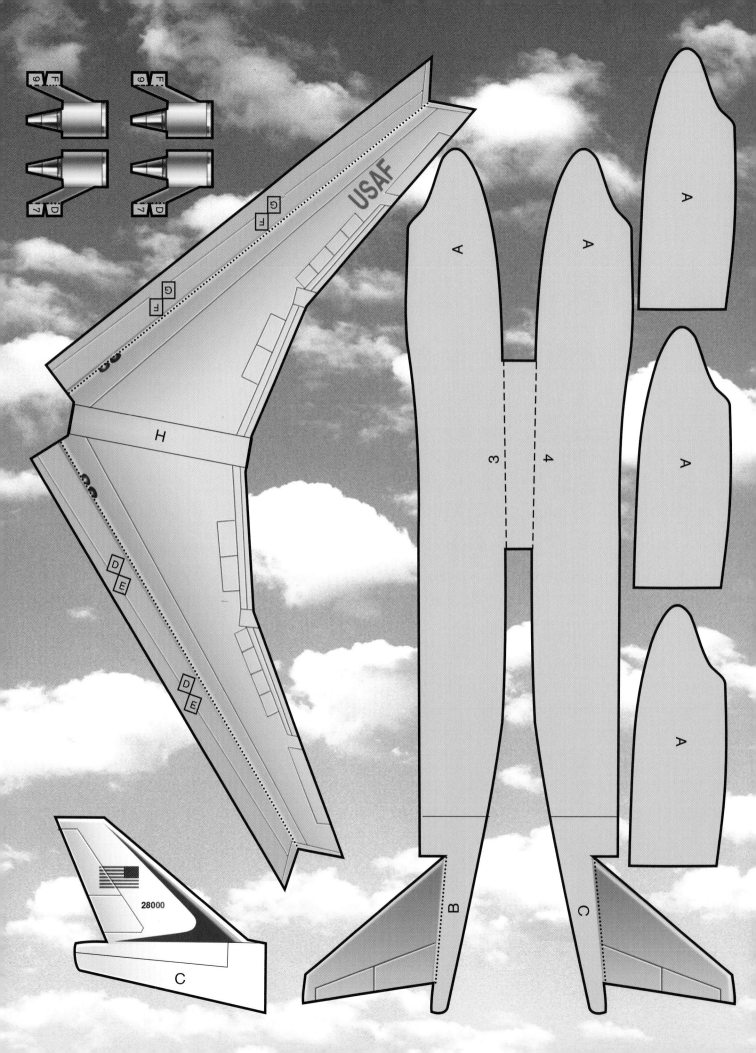

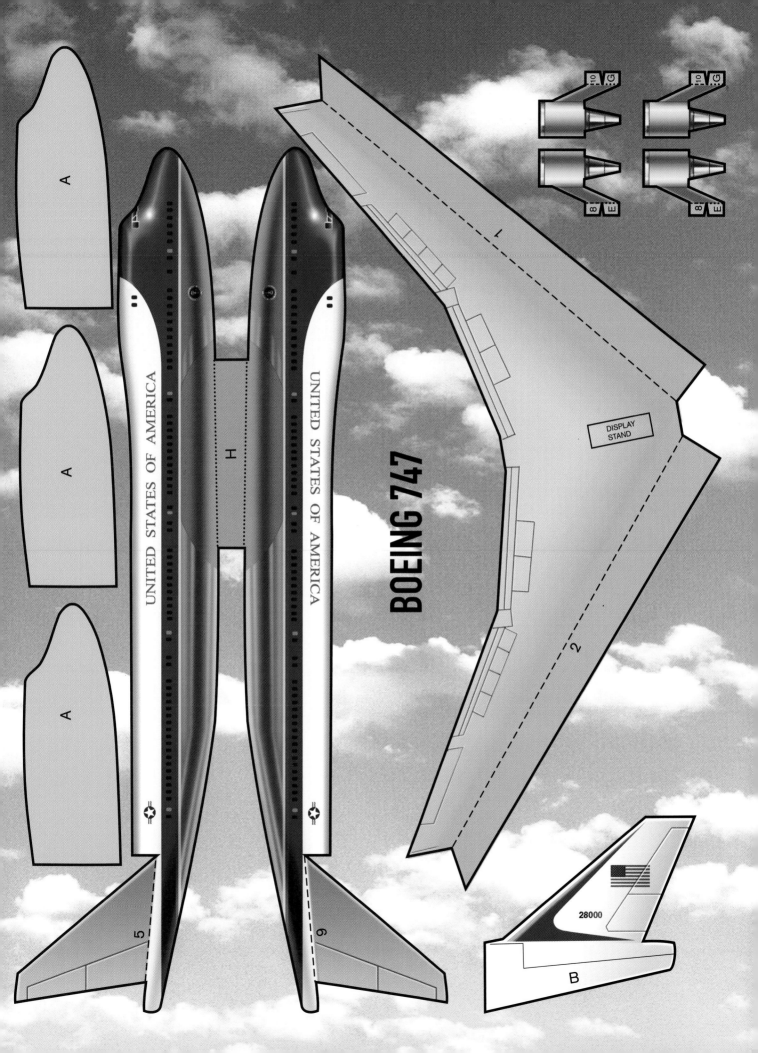

A

A

A

UNITED STATES OF AMERICA

UNITED STATES OF AMERICA

H

BOEING 747

DISPLAY STAND

B

28000

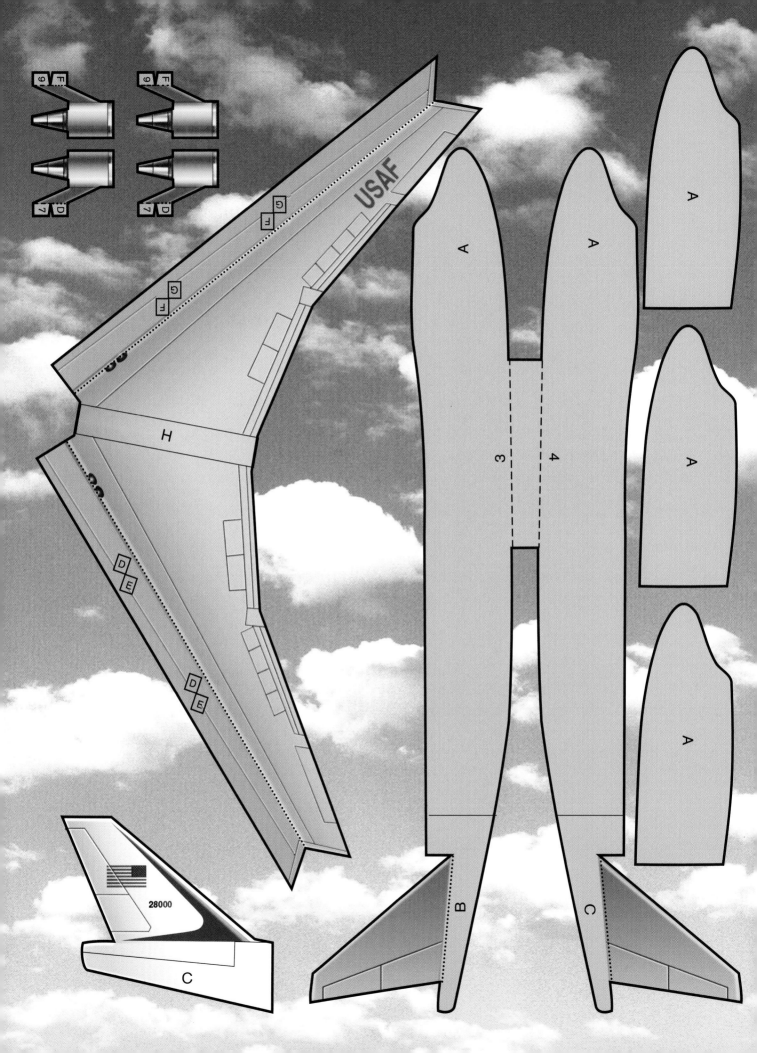

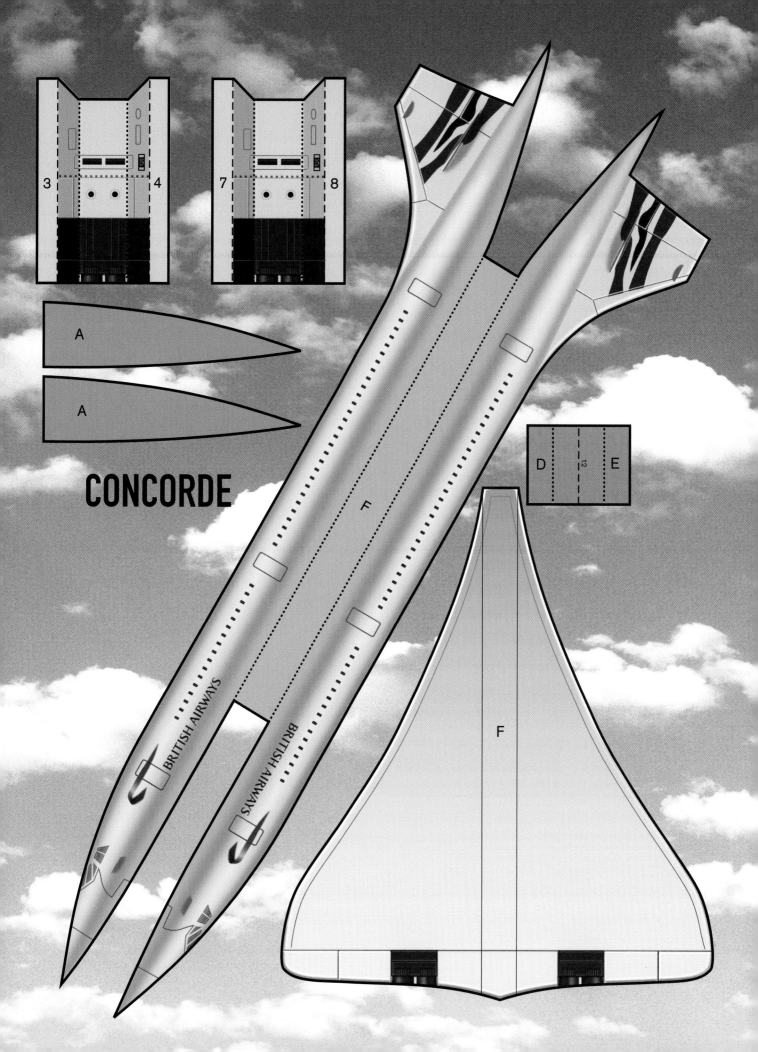

CONCORDE

3   4   7   8

A

A

D   12   E

F

F

BRITISH AIRWAYS

BRITISH AIRWAYS

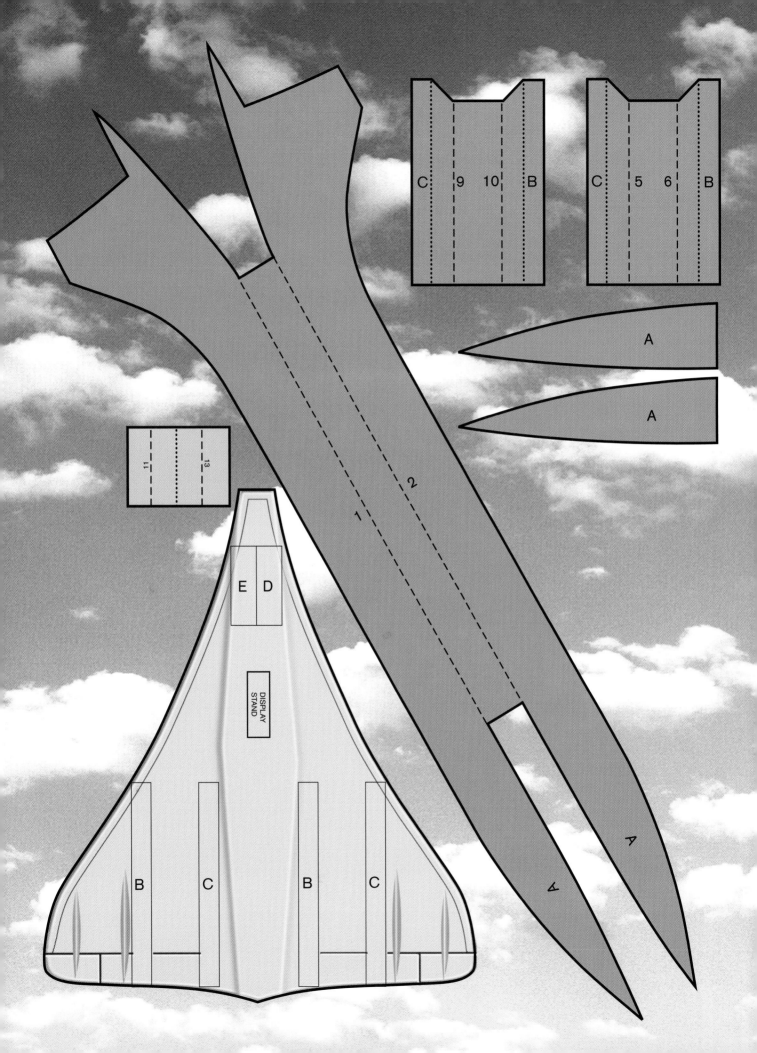

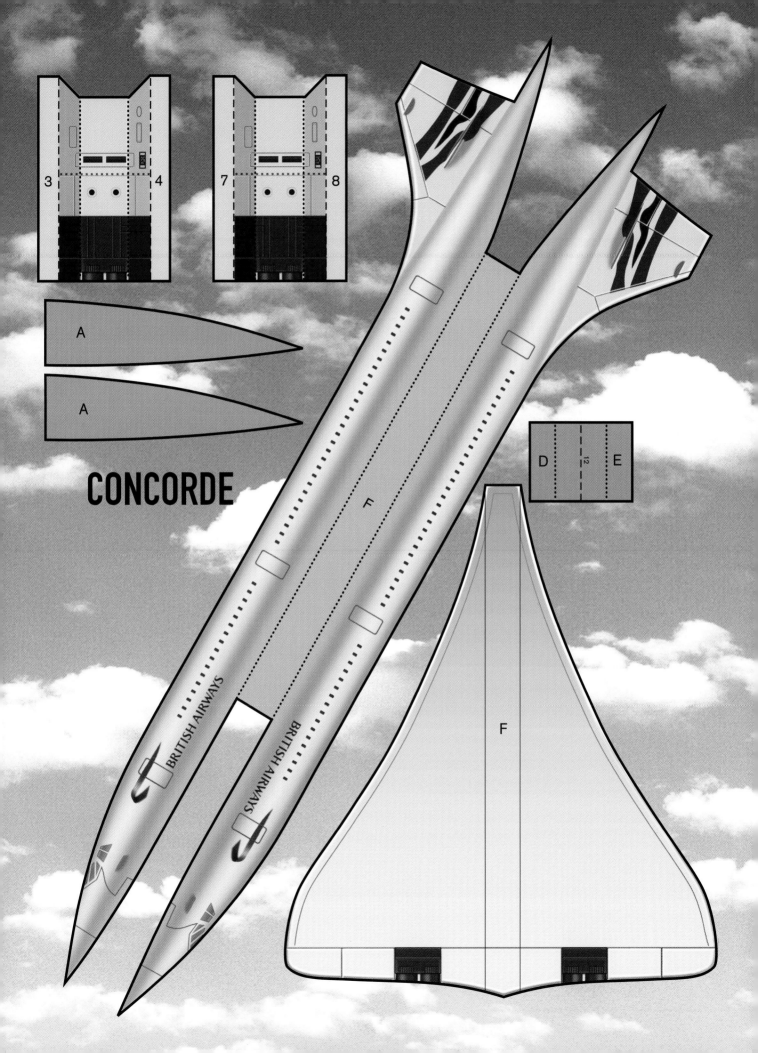

CONCORDE

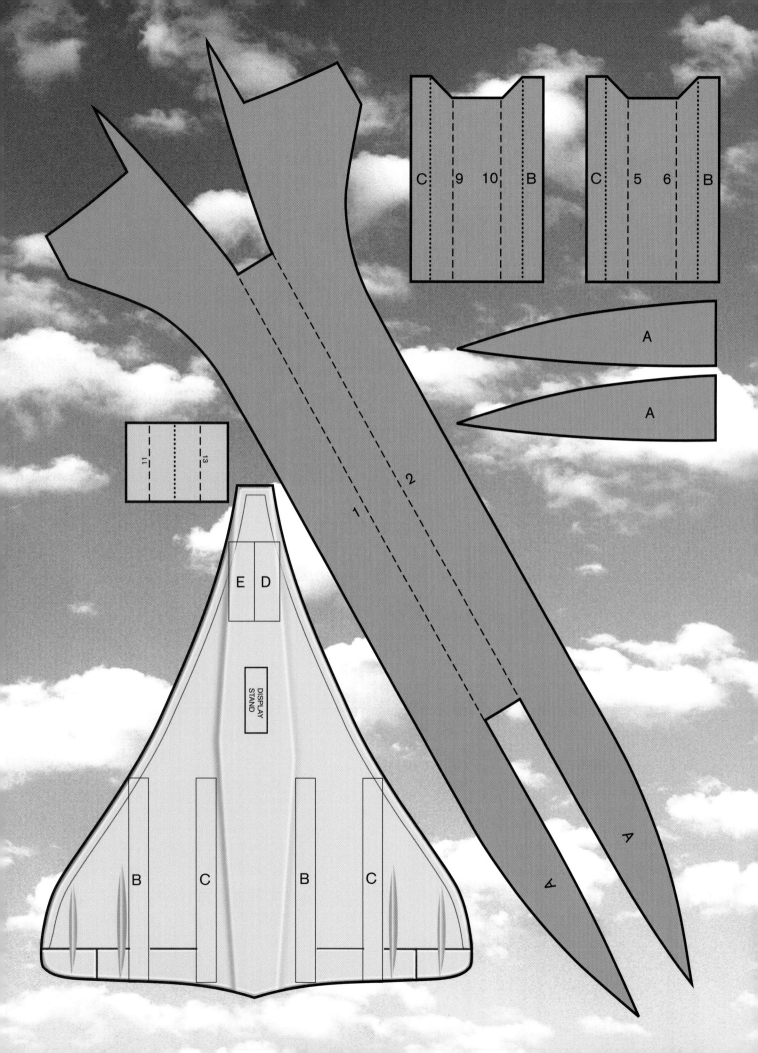

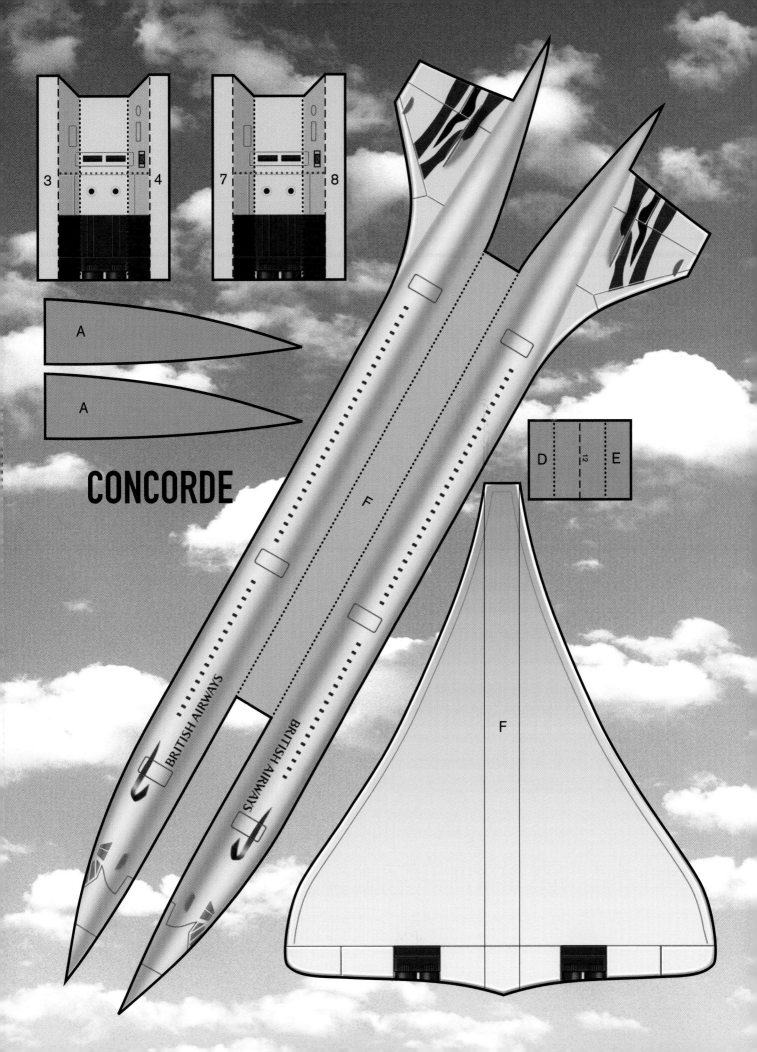

CONCORDE

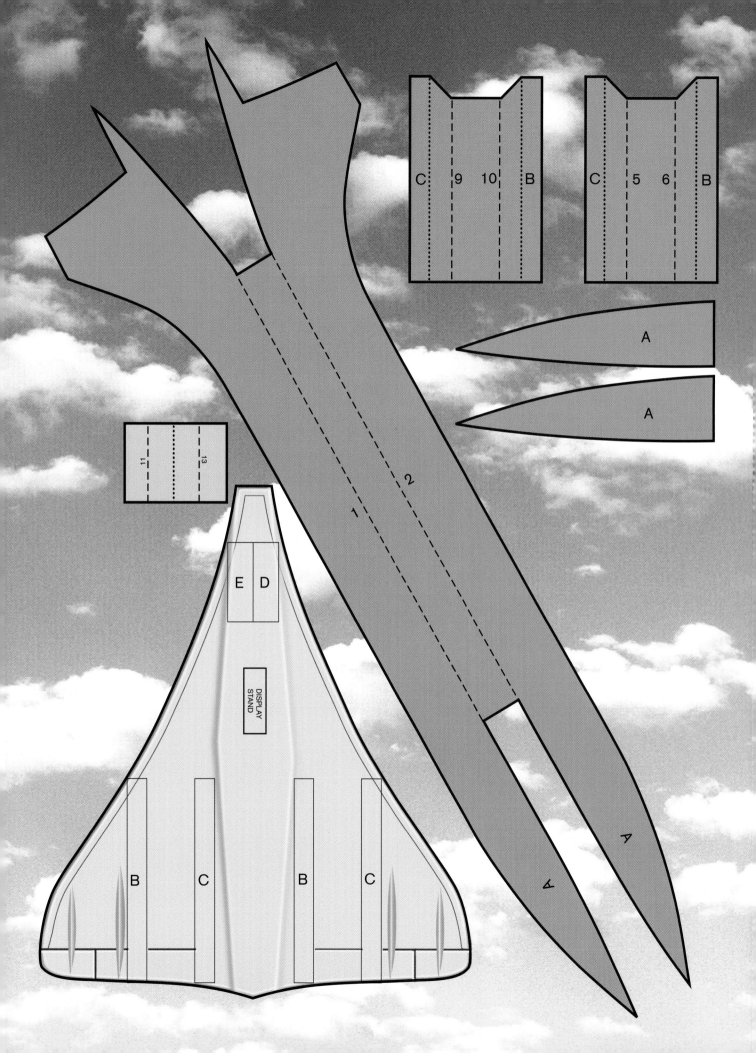

BOEING F-15 EAGLE

BOEING F-15 EAGLE

BOEING F-15 EAGLE

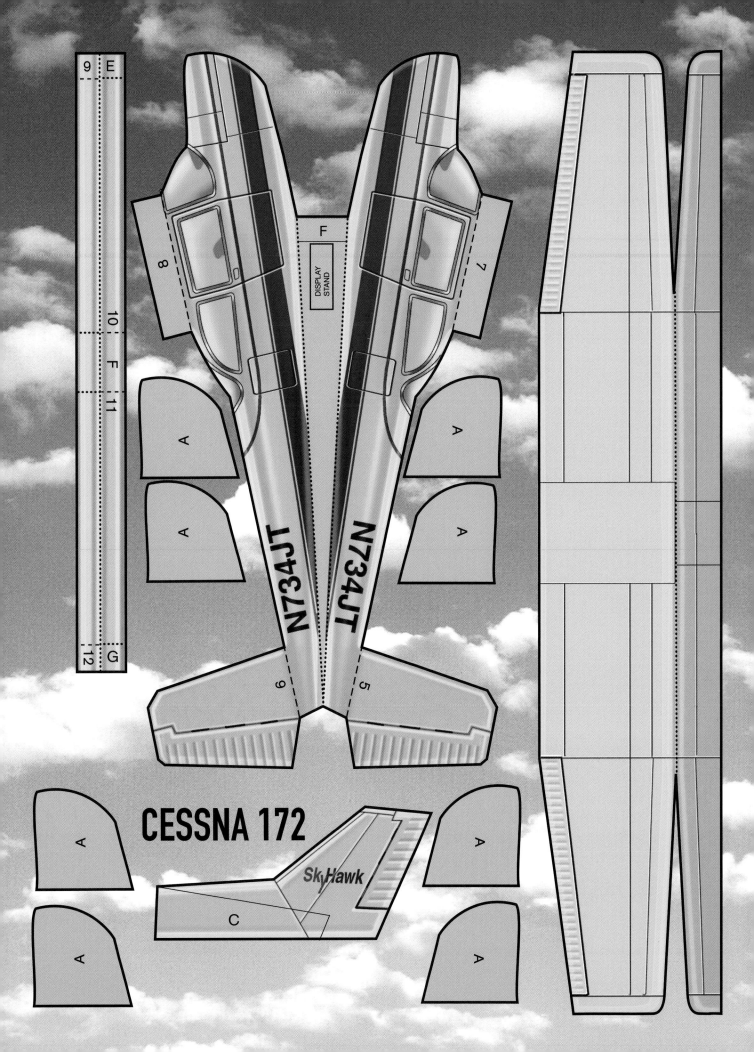

CESSNA 172

N734JT

SkyHawk

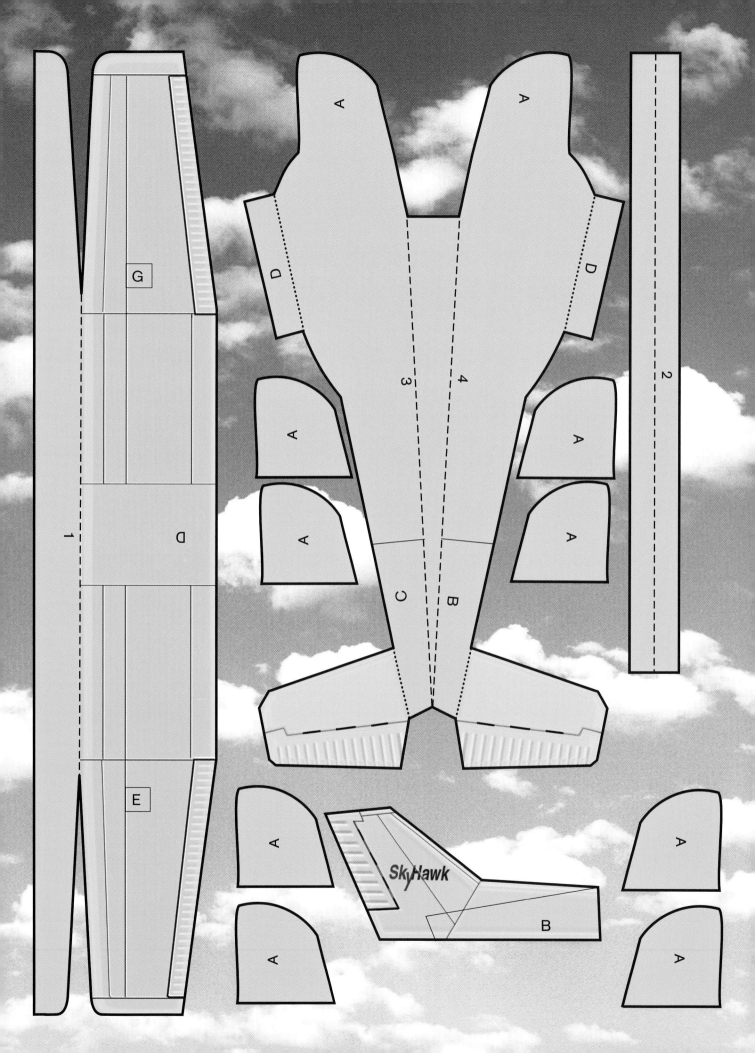

SkyHawk

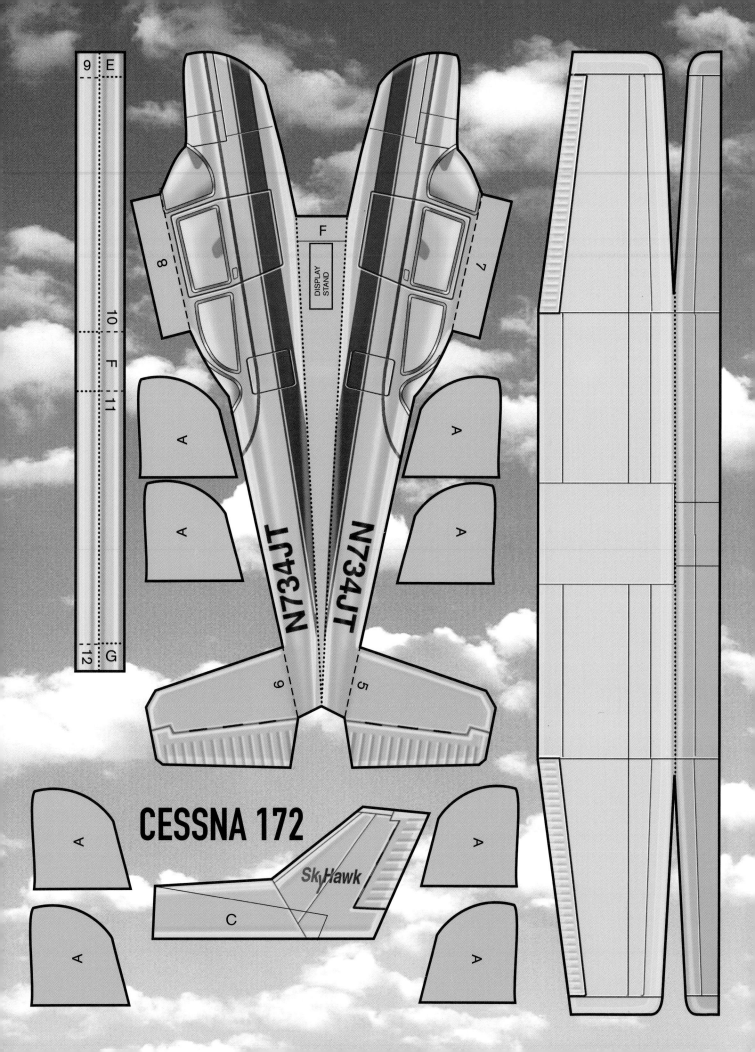

CESSNA 172

N734JT

N734JT

SkyHawk

DISPLAY STAND

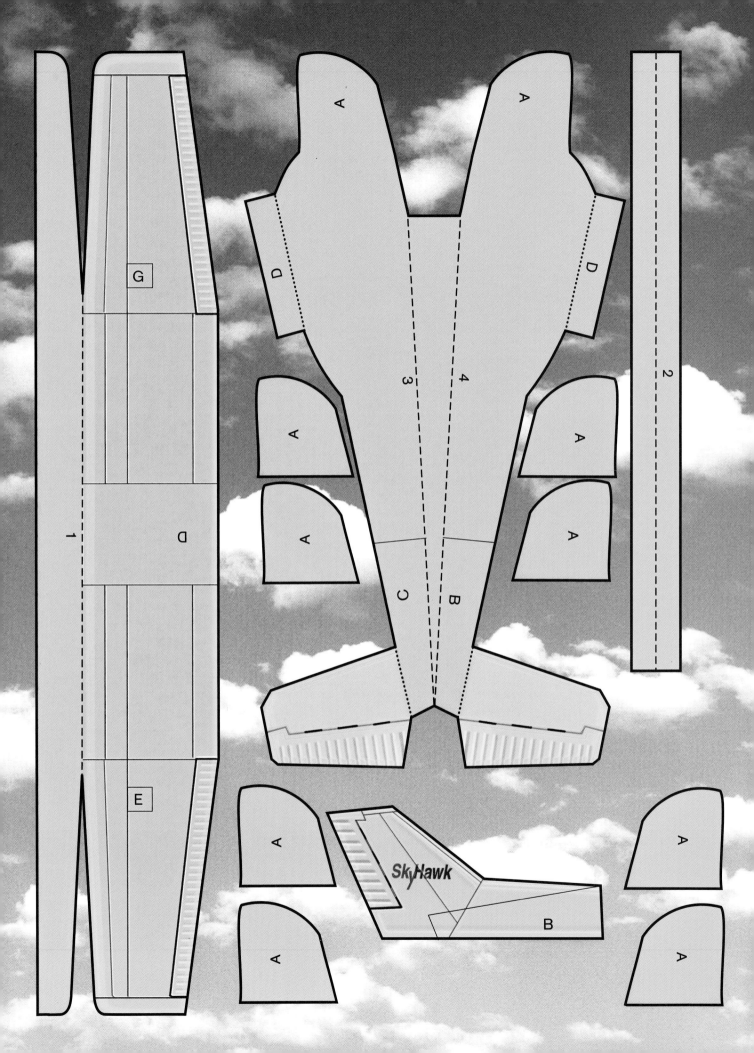

SkyHawk

A

14

DISPLAY STAND

A

G

13

Voyager

B   C

Voyager

N269VA

E   D

N269VA

F   G

D   B   F

RUTAN / YEAGER
VOYAGER

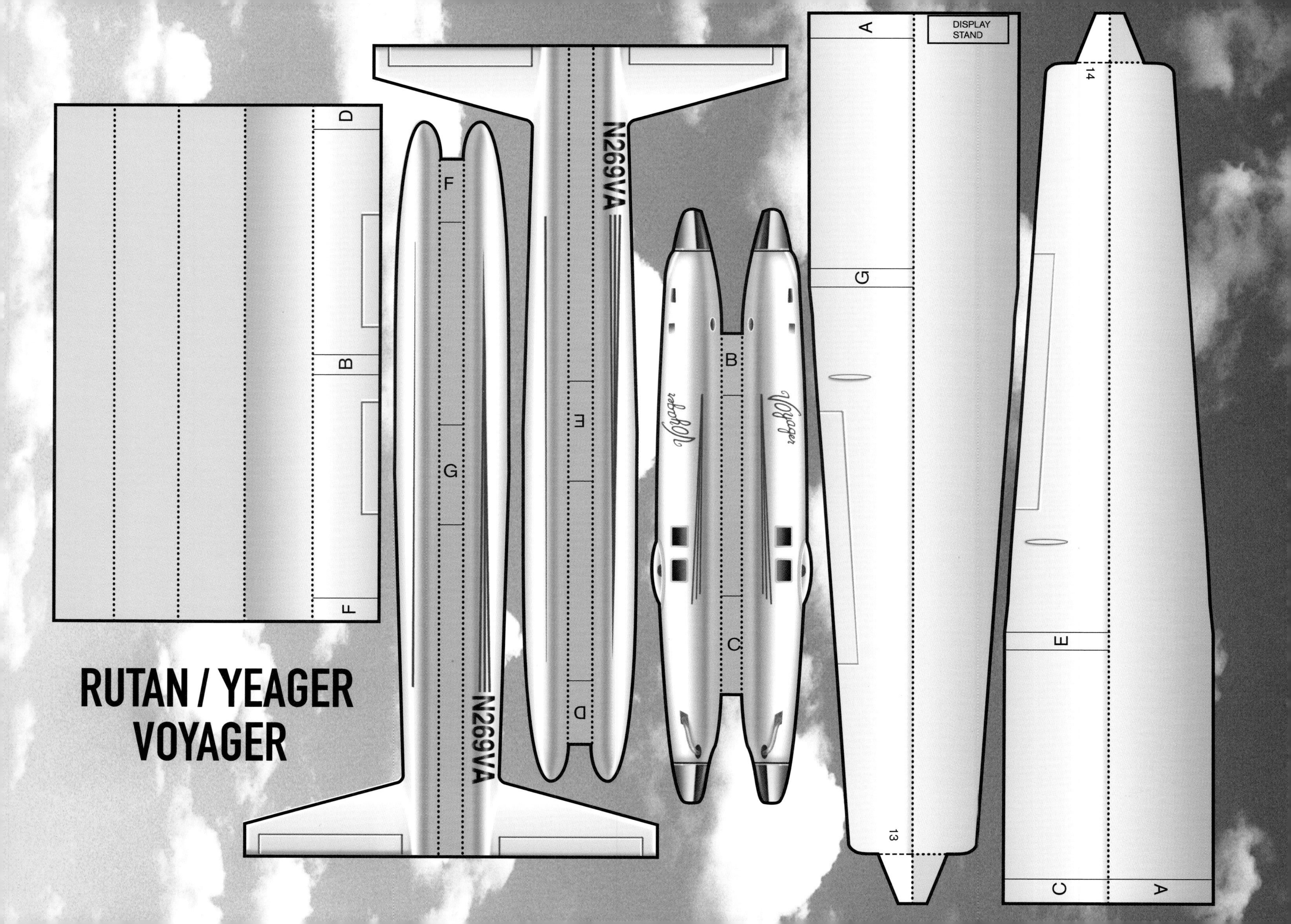

A

14

C

E

DISPLAY
STAND

A

G

13

Voyager

B

C

N269VA

E

D

N269VA

F

G

D

B

F

RUTAN / YEAGER
VOYAGER

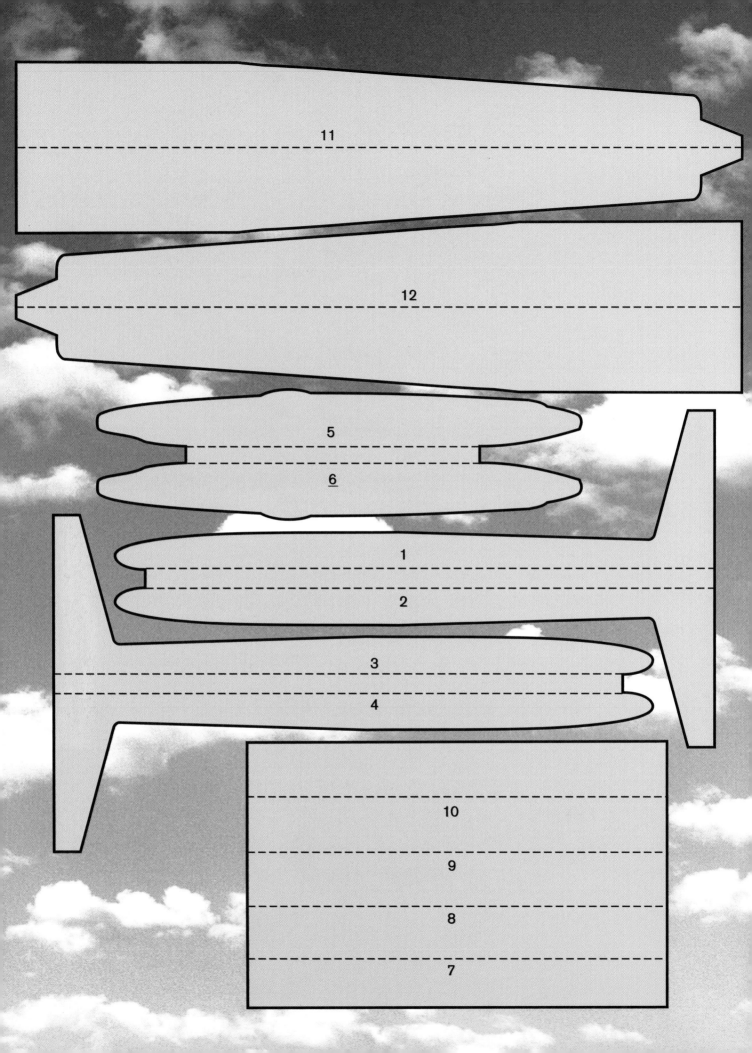

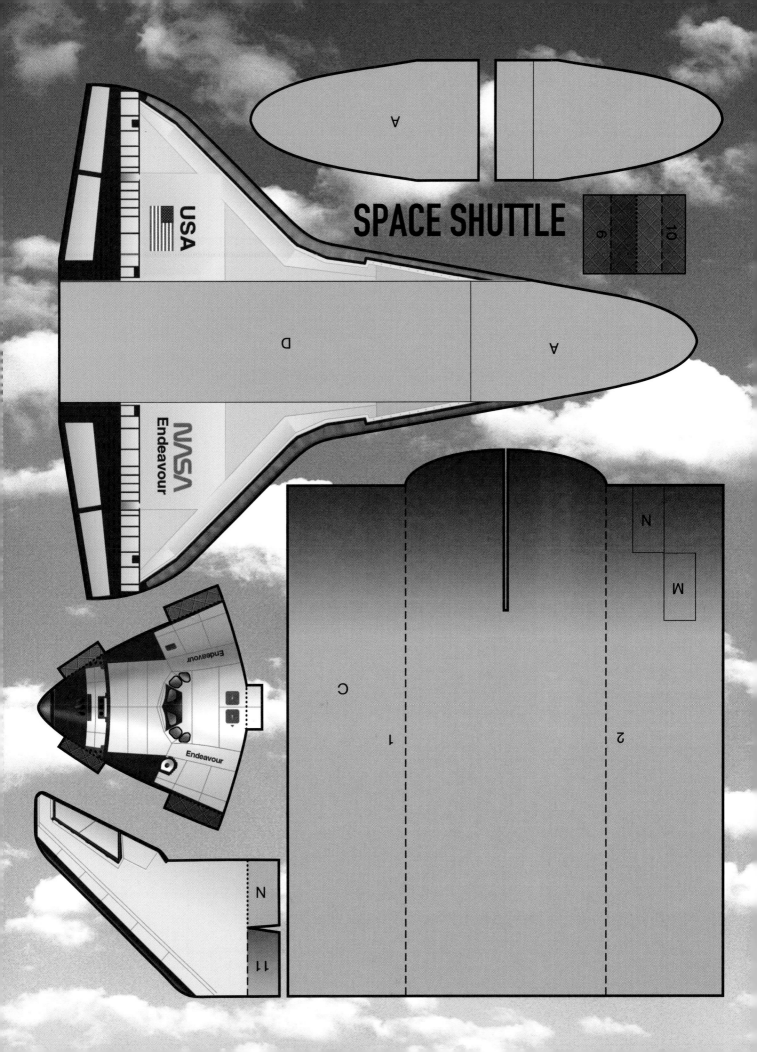

SPACE SHUTTLE

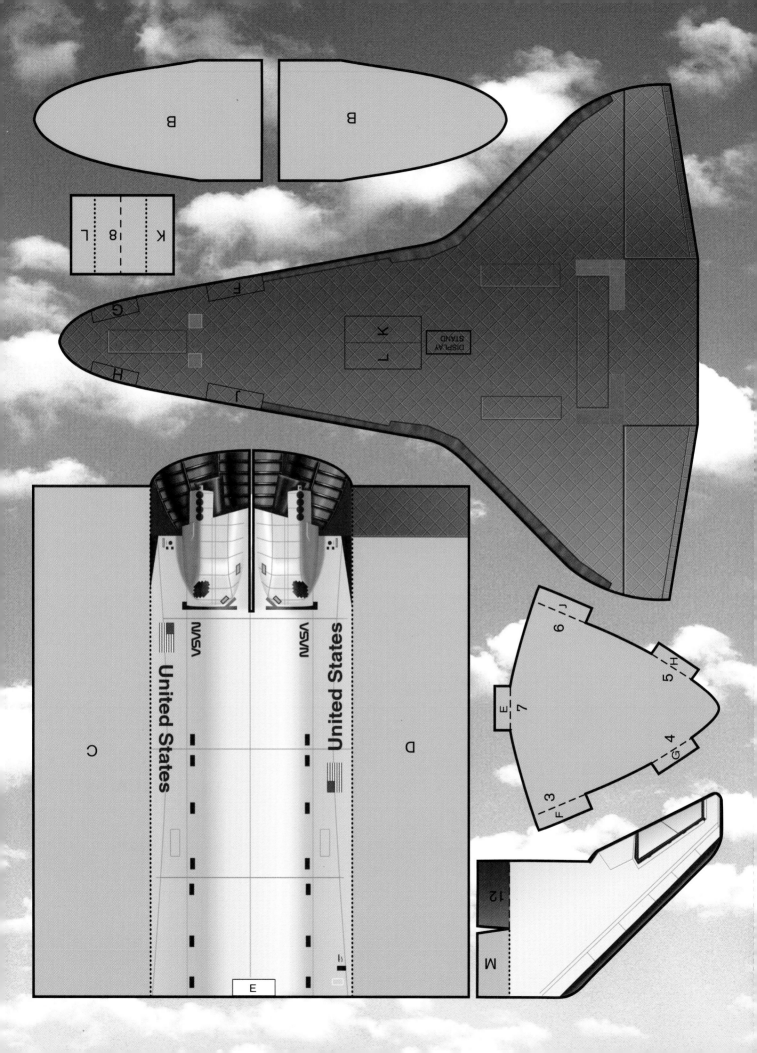

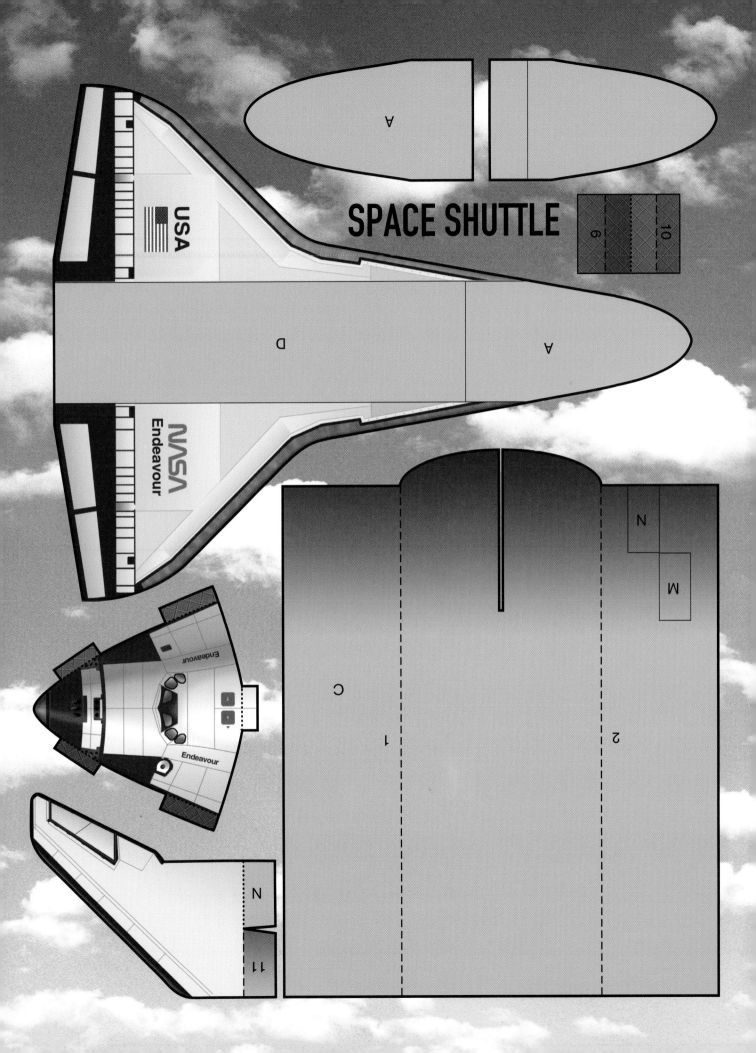

SPACE SHUTTLE

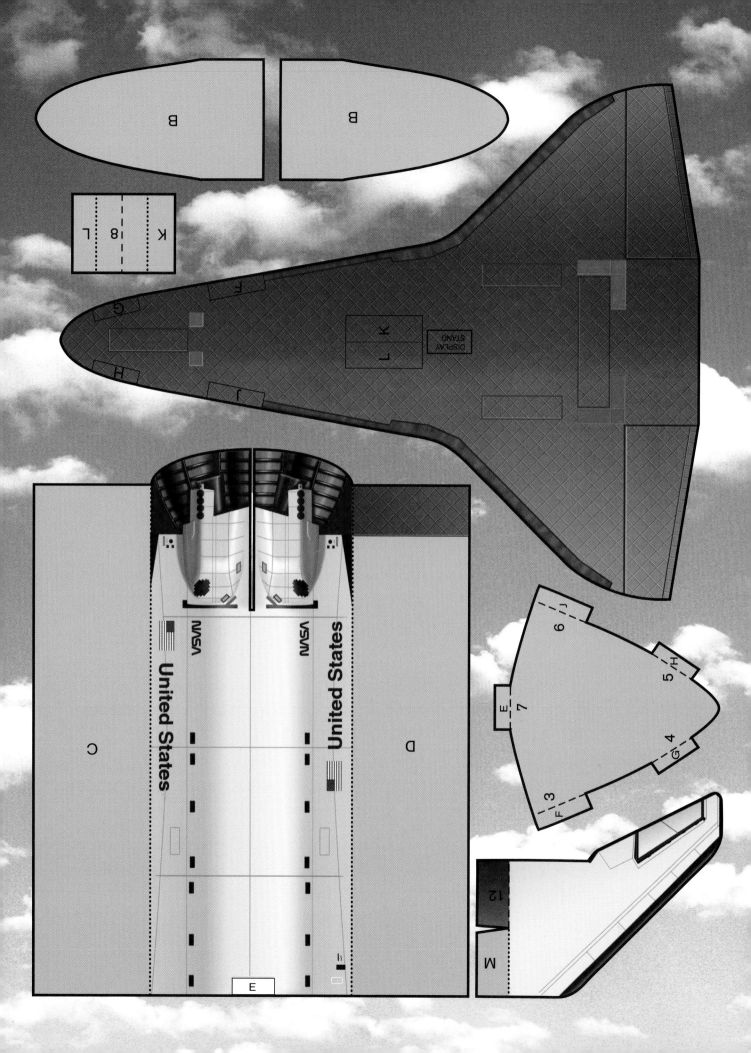

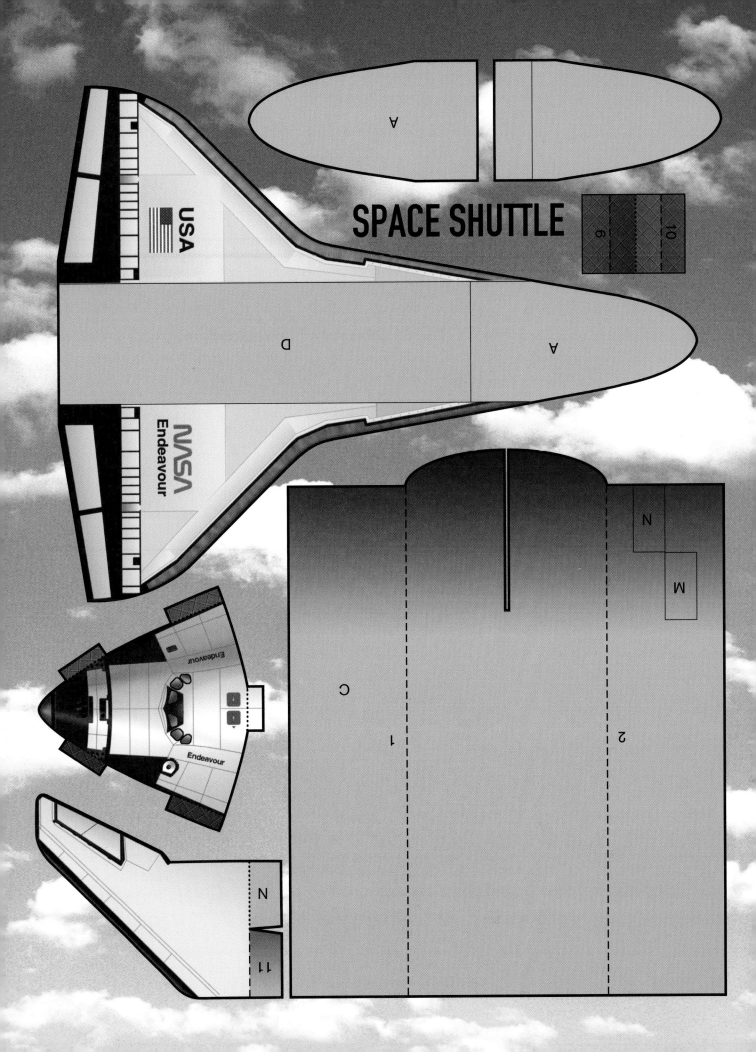

SPACE SHUTTLE

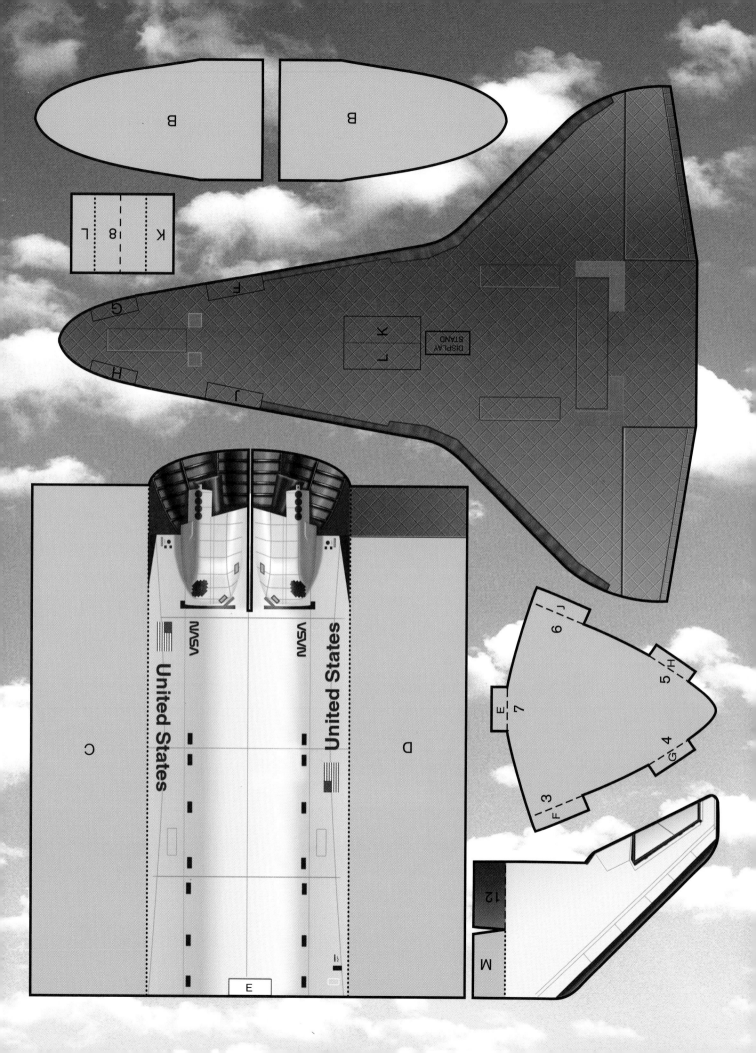

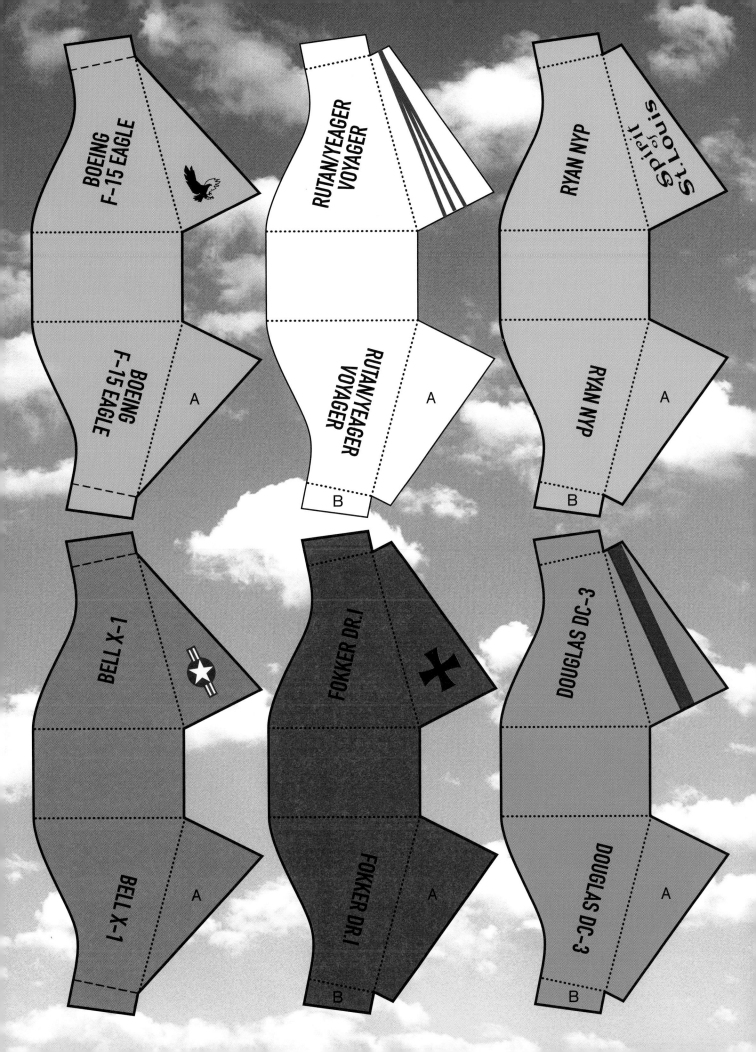

BOEING
F-15 EAGLE

BOEING
F-15 EAGLE

A

RUTAN/YEAGER
VOYAGER

RUTAN/YEAGER
VOYAGER

A

B

RYAN NYP

Spirit
of
St.Louis

RYAN NYP

A

B

BELL X-1

BELL X-1

A

FOKKER DR.I

FOKKER DR.I

A

B

DOUGLAS DC-3

DOUGLAS DC-3

A

B

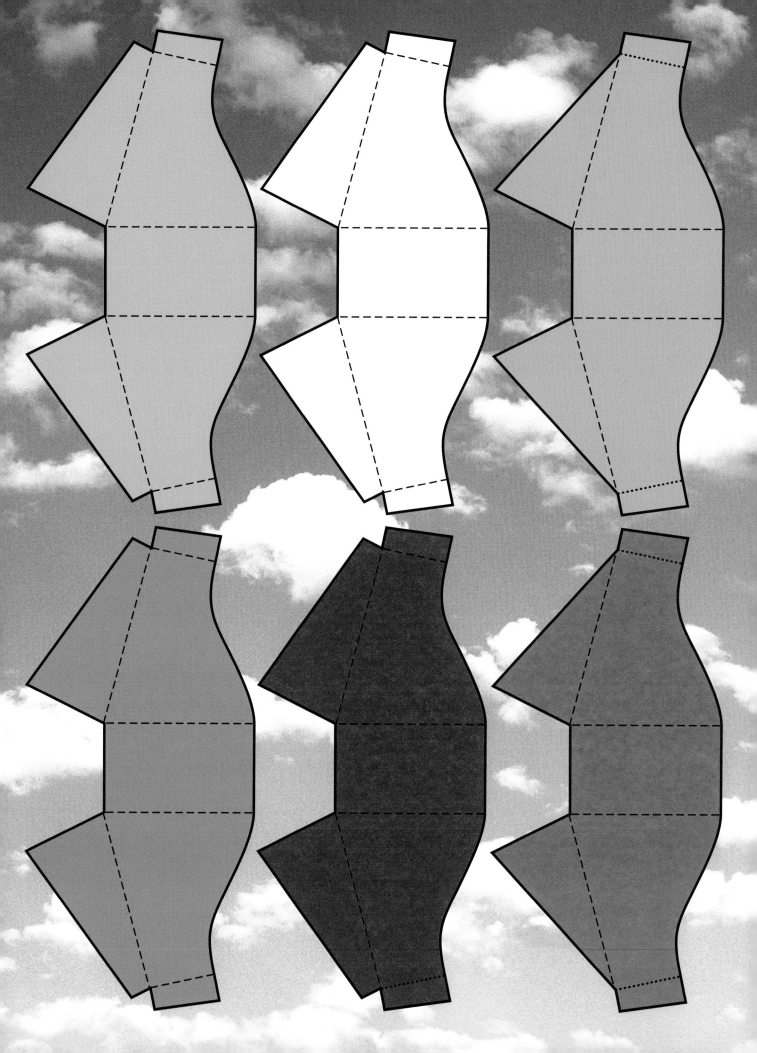

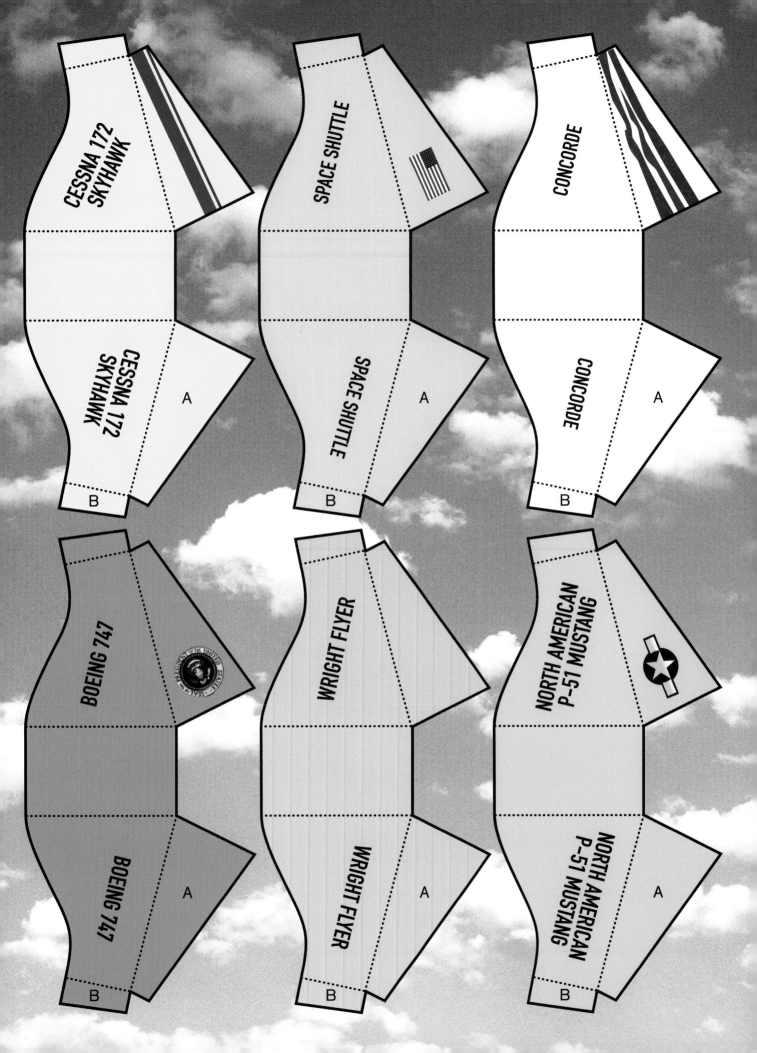

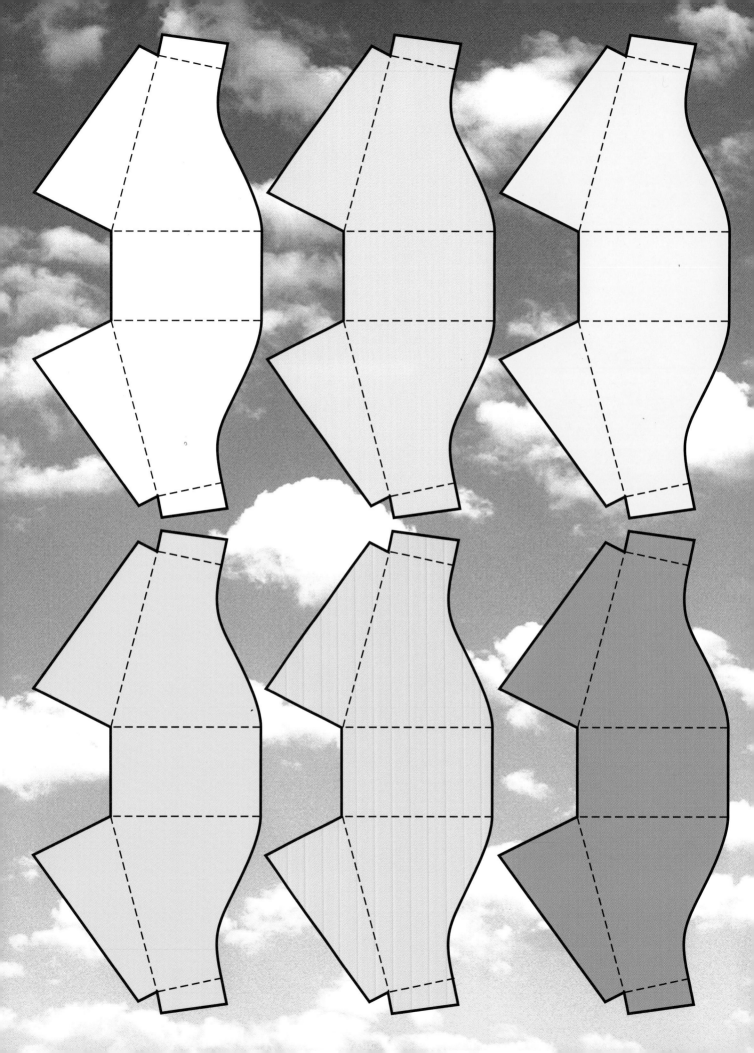